Lecture Notes in Computer Science

Vol. 324: M.P. Chytil, L. Janiga, V. Koubek (Eds.), Mathematical Foundations of Computer Science 1988. Proceedings. IX, 562 pages. 1988.

Vol. 325: G. Brassard, Modern Cryptology. VI, 107 pages. 1988.

Vol. 326: M. Gyssens, J. Paredaens, D. Van Gucht (Eds.), ICDT '88. 2nd International Conference on Database Theory. Proceedings, 1988. VI, 409 pages. 1988.

Vol. 327: G.A. Ford (Ed.), Software Engineering Education. Proceedings, 1988. V, 207 pages. 1988.

Vol. 328: R. Bloomfield, L. Marshall, R. Jones (Eds.), VDM '88. VDM – The Way Ahead. Proceedings, 1988. IX, 499 pages. 1988.

Vol. 329: E. Börger, H. Kleine Büning, M.M. Richter (Eds.), CSL '87. 1st Workshop on Computer Science Logic. Proceedings, 1987. VI, 346 pages. 1988.

Vol. 330: C.G. Günther (Ed.), Advances in Cryptology – EUROCRYPT '88. Proceedings, 1988. XI, 473 pages. 1988.

Vol. 331: M. Joseph (Ed.), Formal Techniques in Real-Time and Fault-Tolerant Systems. Proceedings, 1988. VI, 229 pages. 1988.

Vol. 332: D. Sannella, A. Tarlecki (Eds.), Recent Trends in Data Type Specification. V, 259 pages. 1988.

Vol. 333: H. Noltemeier (Ed.), Computational Geometry and its Applications. Proceedings, 1988. VI, 252 pages. 1988.

Vol. 334: K.R. Dittrich (Ed.), Advances in Object-Oriented Database Systems. Proceedings, 1988. VII, 373 pages. 1988.

Vol. 335: F.A. Vogt (Ed.), CONCURRENCY 88. Proceedings, 1988. VI, 401 pages. 1988.

Vol. 336: B.R. Donald, Error Detection and Recovery in Robotics. XXIV, 314 pages. 1989.

Vol. 337: O. Günther, Efficient Structures for Geometric Data Management. XI, 135 pages. 1988.

Vol. 338: K.V. Nori, S. Kumar (Eds.), Foundations of Software Technology and Theoretical Computer Science. Proceedings, 1988. IX, 520 pages. 1988.

Vol. 339: M. Rafanelli, J.C. Klensin, P. Svensson (Eds.), Statistical and Scientific Database Management, IV SSDBM. Proceedings, 1988. IX, 454 pages. 1989.

Vol. 340: G. Rozenberg (Ed.), Advances in Petri Nets 1988. VI, 439 pages. 1988.

Vol. 341: S. Bittanti (Ed.), Software Reliability Modelling and Identification. VII, 209 pages. 1988.

Vol. 342: G. Wolf, T. Legendi, U. Schendel (Eds.), Parcella '88. Proceedings, 1988. 380 pages. 1989.

Vol. 343: J. Grabowski, P. Lescanne, W. Wechler (Eds.), Algebraic and Logic Programming. Proceedings, 1988. 278 pages. 1988.

Vol. 344: J. van Leeuwen, Graph-Theoretic Concepts in Computer Science. Proceedings, 1988. VII, 459 pages. 1989.

Vol. 345: R.T. Nossum (Ed.), Advanced Topics in Artificial Intelligence. VII, 233 pages. 1988 (Subseries LNAI).

Vol. 346: M. Reinfrank, J. de Kleer, M.L. Ginsberg, E. Sandewall (Eds.), Non-Monotonic Reasoning. Proceedings, 1988. XIV, 237 pages. 1989 (Subseries LNAI).

Vol. 347: K. Morik (Ed.), Knowledge Representation and Organization in Machine Learning. XV, 319 pages. 1989 (Subseries LNAI).

Vol. 348: P. Deransart, B. Lorho, J. Maluszyński (Eds.), Programming Languages Implementation and Logic Programming. Proceedings, 1988. VI, 299 pages. 1989.

Vol. 349: B. Monien, R. Cori (Eds.), STACS 89. Proceedings, 1989. VIII, 544 pages. 1989.

Vol. 350: A. Törn, A. Žilinskas, Global Optimization. X, 255 pages. 1989.

Vol. 351: J. Díaz, F. Orejas (Eds.), TAPSOFT '89. Volume 1. Proceedings, 1989. X, 383 pages. 1989.

Vol. 352: J. Díaz, F. Orejas (Eds.), TAPSOFT '89. Volume 2. Proceedings, 1989. X, 389 pages. 1989.

Vol. 353: S. Hölldobler, Foundations of Equational Logic Programming. X, 250 pages. 1989. (Subseries LNAI).

Vol. 354: J.W. de Bakker, W.-P. de Roever, G. Rozenberg (Eds.), Linear Time, Branching Time and Partial Order in Logics and Models for Concurrency. VIII, 713 pages. 1989.

Vol. 355: N. Dershowitz (Ed.), Rewriting Techniques and Applications. Proceedings, 1989. VII, 579 pages. 1989.

Vol. 356: L. Huguet, A. Poli (Eds.), Applied Algebra, Algebraic Algorithms and Error-Correcting Codes. Proceedings, 1987. VI, 417 pages. 1989.

Vol. 357: T. Mora (Ed.), Applied Algebra, Algebraic Algorithms and Error-Correcting Codes. Proceedings, 1988. IX, 481 pages. 1989.

Vol. 358: P. Gianni (Ed.), Symbolic and Algebraic Computation. Proceedings, 1988. XI, 545 pages. 1989.

Vol. 359: D. Gawlick, M. Haynie, A. Reuter (Eds.), High Performance Transaction Systems. Proceedings, 1987. XII, 329 pages. 1989.

Vol. 360: H. Maurer (Ed.), Computer Assisted Learning – ICCAL '89. Proceedings, 1989. VII, 642 pages. 1989.

Vol. 361: S. Abiteboul, P.C. Fischer, H.-J. Schek (Eds.), Nested Relations and Complex Objects in Databases. VI, 323 pages. 1989.

Vol. 362: B. Lisper, Synthesizing Synchronous Systems by Static Scheduling in Space-Time. VI, 263 pages. 1989.

Vol. 363: A.R. Meyer, M.A. Taitslin (Eds.), Logic at Botik '89. Proceedings, 1989. X, 289 pages. 1989.

Vol. 364: J. Demetrovics, B. Thalheim (Eds.), MFDBS 89. Proceedings, 1989. VI, 428 pages. 1989.

Vol. 365: E. Odijk, M. Rem, J.-C. Syre (Eds.), PARLE '89. Parallel Architectures and Languages Europe. Volume I. Proceedings, 1989. XIII, 478 pages. 1989.

Vol. 366: E. Odijk, M. Rem, J.-C. Syre (Eds.), PARLE '89. Parallel Architectures and Languages Europe. Volume II. Proceedings, 1989. XIII, 442 pages. 1989.

Vol. 367: W. Litwin, H.-J. Schek (Eds.), Foundations of Data Organization and Algorithms. Proceedings, 1989. VIII, 531 pages. 1989.

Vol. 368: H. Boral, P. Faudemay (Eds.), IWDM '89, Database Machines. Proceedings, 1989. VI, 387 pages. 1989.

Vol. 369: D. Taubner, Finite Representations of CCS and TCSP Programs by Automata and Petri Nets. X. 168 pages. 1989.

Vol. 370: Ch. Meinel, Modified Branching Programs and Their Computational Power. VI, 132 pages. 1989.

Vol. 371: D. Hammer (Ed.), Compiler Compilers and High Speed Compilation. Proceedings, 1988. VI, 242 pages. 1989.

Vol. 372: G. Ausiello, M. Dezani-Ciancaglini, S. Ronchi Della Rocca (Eds.), Automata, Languages and Programming. Proceedings, 1989. XI, 788 pages. 1989.

Vol. 373: T. Theoharis, Algorithms for Parallel Polygon Rendering. VIII, 147 pages. 1989.

Vol. 374: K.A. Robbins, S. Robbins, The Cray X-MP/Model 24. VI, 165 pages. 1989.

Vol. 375: J.L.A. van de Snepscheut (Ed.), Mathematics of Program Construction. Proceedings, 1989. VI, 421 pages. 1989.

Vol. 376: N.E. Gibbs (Ed.), Software Engineering Education. Proceedings, 1989. VII, 312 pages. 1989.

Vol. 377: M. Gross, D. Perrin (Eds.), Electronic Dictionaries and Automata in Computational Linguistics. Proceedings, 1987. V, 110 pages. 1989.

Vol. 378: J.H. Davenport (Ed.), EUROCAL '87. Proceedings, 1987. VIII, 499 pages. 1989.

Lecture Notes in Computer Science

Edited by G. Goos and J. Hartmanis

423

Lionel E. Deimel (Ed.)

Software Engineering Education

SEI Conference 1990
Pittsburgh, Pennsylvania, USA, April 2–3, 1990
Proceedings

Springer-Verlag

Berlin Heidelberg New York London Paris Tokyo Hong Kong

Volume Editor

Lionel E. Deimel
Software Engineering Institute, Carnegie Mellon University
Pittsburgh, PA 15213, USA

Carnegie Mellon University
Software Engineering Institute

CR Subject Classification (1987): D.2, K.3.2

ISBN 0-387-97274-9 Springer-Verlag New York Berlin Heidelberg
ISBN 3-540-97274-9 Springer-Verlag Berlin Heidelberg New York

Printing and binding: Druckhaus Beltz, Hemsbach/Bergstr.
2145/3140-543210 – Printed on acid-free paper

Preface

This volume is the proceedings of *CSEE '90*, the 4th *SEI Conference on Software Engineering Education*, held in Pittsburgh, Pennsylvania April 2 and 3, 1990. This annual conference is sponsored by the Education Program of the Software Engineering Institute (SEI), a federally funded research and development center sponsored by the U.S. Department of Defense and operated by Carnegie Mellon University. The conference provides a forum for discussion of software engineering education and training among members of the academic, industry, and government communities.

The 12 papers chosen for presentation at *CSEE '90* were selected from 28 submitted for consideration. The authors of several papers describing particular graduate programs were asked to participate in a panel on graduate programs in software engineering. Brief descriptions of their programs are also included here, as are position papers by members of a panel on industry-university cooperation and an abstract of the keynote address by Professor David Gries.

Selection of papers was done by a Program Committee from the SEI:

> Mark Ardis
> Maribeth Carpenter
> Gary Ford
> Harvey Hallman
> James Tomayko

In addition to the above people, the following were referees:

Len Bass, *SEI*
Judy Bamberger, *SEI*
Daniel Berry, *Technion*
Richard Fairley, *George Mason University*
Robert Firth, *SEI*
Gretchen Forbes, *Digital Equipment Corp.*
William Frakes, *Software Productivity Consortium*
Norman Gibbs, *SEI*
John Gilligan, *U.S. Air Force*
Robert Goldberg, *IBM Corp.*
John Knight, *University of Virginia*
Jeffrey Lasky, *Rochester Institute of Technology*
Everald Mills, *Seattle University*
John Musa, *AT&T Bell Laboratories*
George Smith, *Motorola Inc.*
Scott Stevens, *SEI*

Steven Wartik, *Software Productivity Consortium*
Nelson Weiderman, *SEI*
Richard Weis, *University of Hawaii, Hilo*
Robert Winner, *Institute for Defense Analyses*

I would like to express my thanks to the Program Committee and referees, and to Angela Wilkerson and especially Mary Rose Serafini, who helped with administrative details and who kept this whole project on schedule.

Lionel E. Deimel
CSEE '90 Program Chairman

Pittsburgh, Pennsylvania
December 1989

CONTENTS

KEYNOTE ADDRESS:

Instilling Professionalism in Software Engineers
David Gries, Cornell University 1

PAPERS:

Establishing Motorola-University Relationships: A
Software Engineering Training Perspective 2
George Sanders and George Smith, Motorola Inc.

Technology Transfer: The Design, Development, and
Implementation of a Process 13
Rebecca L. Smith, Hewlett-Packard Co.

An Undergraduate Curriculum in Software Engineering 24
Harlan D. Mills, J. R. Newman, and C. B. Engle, Jr., Florida Institute
of Technology

An Undergraduate Programme in Software Engineering 38
M. F. Bott, University College of Wales

An Undergraduate Software Engineering Major Embedded
in a Computer Systems Engineering Degree 49
K. Reed and T. S. Dillon, La Trobe University

Introduction of Software Engineering Concepts in an
Ada-Based Introductory Computer Science Course 67
Frances L. Van Scoy, West Virginia University

Teaching Reuse Early 77
Viswa Santhanam, Boeing Military Airplanes

A State-of-the-Art CS Undergraduate Lab 85
J. Mack Adams and Barry L. Kurtz, New Mexico State University

--StarLite-- A Software Education Laboratory 95
Robert P. Cook and Lifeng Hsu, University of Virginia

Modeling Teamwork in an Academic Environment 110
J. P. Jacquot and J. Guyard, Université de Nancy I
L. Boidot, CEGELEC/RED

An Experience of Teaching Concurrency:
looking back, looking forward 123
David Bustard, Queen's University, Belfast

Use-Perspective Unit Documentation 136
Frank A. Cioch and Fatma Mili, Oakland University

PANEL DISCUSSIONS:

Graduate Programs in Software Engineering 145

Moderator: *Gary Ford, Software Engineering Institute, CMU*

Panelists: *Alfs Berztiss, University of Pittsburgh*
Daniel R. Bidwell, Andrews University
Bernice M. Folz, College of St. Thomas
Norman E. Gibbs, Software Engineering Institute, CMU
Daniel Olivier, Intermetrics, Inc.

**Industry-Academic Cooperation in Software Engineering Training
and Continuing Education** 157

Moderator: *George Smith, Motorola Inc.*

Panelists: *Dr. A. Frank Ackerman, AT&T Bell Laboratories*
George N. Arnovick, California State University, Chico
W. J. "Gus" Radzyminski, Eastman Kodak Company
George Sanders, Motorola Inc.

KEYNOTE ADDRESS:
Instilling Professionalism in Software Engineers

David Gries
Cornell University

Abstract. *I believe it is fair to say that software engineering, as a whole, does not display the same high "professional" attitudes that one finds in other engineering fields. For example, software engineers don't demand (of themselves) the same degree of rigor and clarity in their contracts (specifications) with clients that one finds in other engineering fields. The design, programming, and testing of programs and software systems often take far too long. Programs are usually difficult to understand, leading to the high cost of "maintenance." And few software products bear the guarantee of their authors that the product is correct—in fact, much software comes with a complete disclaimer as to the responsibility of its author!*

The reasons for this situation will be discussed, and some avenues of rectifying it will be explored.

Establishing Motorola-University Relationships:
A Software Engineering Training Perspective

George Sanders and George Smith
Motorola Inc.

Abstract. *Motorola requires a skilled software engineering work force to accommodate the growing importance of software within our products and our corporation. The current computer science curricula at most universities do not prepare students to develop industrial strength software and little is available in the way of continuing professional development. Consequently, Motorola has begun a major initiative to develop and deliver software engineering training. This paper discusses Motorola's effort to establish the training needs of its software engineers and the results of that effort. It provides conclusions from the ongoing investigation of other major companies' software engineering training. It contrasts industry-university relationships in the US, Japan, and Europe. Finally, it discusses the establishment of Motorola-university training programs in the United States, Israel, and Japan.*

1. Introduction

Motorola requires, as a corporate policy, that every employee receives a minimum of 40 hours of training per year. This commitment to training is equally expressed in our growing software engineering training program.

Unlike some other organizations, Motorola, with few exceptions, does not have a full time training staff dedicated to software engineering. As the size and scope of the software demand increases, those key software developers who could be called upon to teach become less available because their expertise has simultaneously become more valuable to both their software development project and the Motorola training community. It is apparent that Motorola-university cooperation in the training of software engineers must play a key role in meeting our software engineering training needs.

2. DACUM

In order to provide the appropriate software engineering training to our engineers, it first became necessary to identify the courses our engineers needed to improve their performance in the workplace.. Unlike general education, industrial training must provide the student with the correct job skills mix that will be used on the job. To begin our curriculum development efforts, Motorola chose to use a curriculum development model called DACUM (Developing a Curriculum) offered by Ohio State University. DACUM is an innovative approach to occupational analysis. It has proven to be a very effective method of quickly determining, at relatively low cost, the tasks that must be performed by persons employed in a given occupational area.

The job model that results from the DACUM analysis is a detailed and graphic portrayal of the duties and tasks involved in the occupation or job studied. Motorola has developed six software engineering models as part of a corporate-wide analysis, including software engineer, senior-level software engineer, software project management, and team leader.

DACUM operates on the following premises:

Expert workers are able to describe/define their jobs better than anyone else.

Any job can be effectively and sufficiently described in terms of the tasks that successful workers in that occupation perform.

Based on this analysis, Motorola concluded that the software engineering process is basically culturally independent. Software engineers across the country as well as around the world perform the same set of tasks. In a training context, this indicated that a set of training courses that are appropriate in one location (e.g., domestic U.S.) will be appropriate in other locations.

Differences do exist in the area of people management and interpersonal skills requirements. They also exist in the area of labor relations and legal issues. These courses must be tailored to a particular geographic location, if not specially developed to address the peculiar needs. In addition, depending on the specific product or customer, certain processes or procedures must be followed. These product or customer requirements indicated the need for specific training to meet these needs. Also, those software engineers who develop large systems are much more dependent on the software development process for achieving high quality and productivity. This process dependency is representative of a higher level of sophistication of the software engineers. Training in these product areas requires more sophistication than that aimed at smaller product developers.

The following list of training-related topics represents data taken from the six job models completed to date. The list represents a starting point from which training development activity can begin. Each topic is briefly annotated with a description of the training need as determined by the analysis.

Software Engineering Basics. As a prerequisite to further training and development, this topic consists of at least seven fundamental courses in software development:

- Discrete Mathematics
- Computer Architecture
- Operating Systems Theory
- Concepts in Programming
- Programming Languages
- Data Structure Design
- Algorithm Design

Project Management. In each of the job models, project management appears as a major duty. Panelists identified project management as an activity in which training would significantly improve software engineering performance and productivity. Panelists identified size estimation, budget management, cost-benefit analysis, project tracking, and risk management as tasks within project management that require training intervention.

Software Design. Based on our job model, software design emerged as a major duty requiring training. Specific issues within design involve timing, embedded software, enhancement, structure charts, module specifications, and process allocation.

Advanced C. Both managers and software engineers identified language knowledge and skills as important to the successful performance of their jobs.

C++. Both managers and software engineers identified language knowledge and skills as important to the successful performance of their jobs.

Configuration Management. Identified by panelists as a training need in the areas of version and change control and metrics collection.

Reusability. Panelists discussed reusability in many of the duties and tasks they identified, from project planning to product maintenance. Reusability appeared as an area of concern for both managers and software engineers, and is an essential ingredient toward improved quality and productivity.

Digital Signal Processing. Digital Signal Processing appears as an emerging industrial technology.

Artificial Intelligence. Identified as an emerging industrial technology.

Orientation. Similar to existing orientation programs, but tailored to the entry-level software engineer.

Testing. Testing appeared as a major duty in the software engineer's job model. Several of the specific tasks within this duty requiring training intervention include generating test plans and performing module, integration, system, and acceptance tests.

Metrics. Using metrics consistently appeared as tasks for both the manager and software engineer. Specific tasks identified as requiring training intervention include writing statistics collection plans, defining, collecting, and analyzing metrics, feeding back metrics analysis to the process, and defining project performance measurement techniques.

Reviews. Reviews appeared at many points in the job model. Specific training needs include participating in walkthroughs, validating design and code, critiquing designs for technical content, and preparing and presenting post mortems.

Other areas of software development identified through the job models include:

- Ada
- Software Process Development and Improvement
- Software Reliability
- Real Time Executives
- UNIX^{TM}
- Software Quality
- Verification and Validation
- Standards and Procedures
- System Engineering
- Object-oriented Design
- Legal Issues
- Expert Systems
- Entry Level Training Program

The DACUM process provided a very high level profile of the software engineering population within Motorola. Additional work is required to develop a more detailed profile of the sub-populations within the software engineering community, e.g., software quality assurance, management information systems, etc.

Finally, the high level profile has assisted Motorola in the development of a preliminary "curriculum road map" from which more detailed and specific courses can be developed. This work is on-going in Motorola. The DACUM analysis identifies the areas in which training is required. The benchmarking process discussed below provides Motorola with information about how other organizations have succeeded in meeting these same needs.

By analyzing the differences among the six software engineering models developed using the DACUM process, we have concluded that while there are universal skills required of a software engineer, each organization has a skill set specific to their organization and product. Anyone interested in using the DACUM process should contact The National Center for Research in Vocational Education at Ohio State University.

3. Training Benchmarking

Benchmarking is an ongoing activity within Motorola and is not limited to software engineering training. Motorola benchmarking is characterized as a sharing of information among industrial organizations with similar needs. Every large organization has pockets of excellence within it. These benchmarking activities seek out these pockets of excellence. Motorola uses the lessons learned within its own organization to improve our software engineering training. Motorola also shares information with the companies it benchmarks, thus creating better software engineering education in both organizations.

Below is a summary of our benchmarking findings to date. The information is expressed in ranges of data to maintain the confidentiality of the individual companies we visited. The information is based on structured interviews with members of several "best-in-class" companies.

- Number of software developers:
  4,000 to 20,000
- Type of Curriculum in Place:
  Mature/Rigid to Proposed
- Number of Hours per Year:
  20 Suggested to 40 Minimum Mandated
- Number of Courses Offered:
  3.5 to 400
- Number of Instructional Designers:
  0 to 20

- In-house Instructional Staff:
  0 to 100
- Contract Instructional Staff:
  3 to 50 (estimated)
- Training Media:
  Instructor-led to All Types
- Funding:
  Charge-backs to Allocation

4. Software Engineering Benchmarking

Motorola has undertaken a world-wide benchmarking activity to understand better how other companies throughout the world develop software. Like the training benchmarking, this activity is characterized by a sharing of information with the companies we benchmark. This section contains only that information which is relative to software engineering training based on our understanding of the information provided.

Benchmarking in Japan has revealed a different industry-university relationship than that which exists in the U.S. Japanese companies do not generally look to the universities for support of their software engineering training needs. The general reason seems to be that their organizational objectives are quite different. In order of priority, the universities are perceived by industry to prepare students to first, become university professors, second, become government civil servants, and third, work in industry. Some respondents even went as far as to characterize industry employees who returned to work in universities as "selling out" the company. The reader is cautioned not to draw conclusions from these statements as they may not be representative of the overall situation in Japan. But for whatever reason, Japanese companies have undertaken extensive in-house training activities ranging from cultural indoctrination to specific skill development consisting of several weeks initially and up to 10% or 15% annually of engineers' time.

The Japanese company has one advantage over the U.S. company. The newly hired Japanese software engineers are well trained in the use of statistics. This greatly facilitates the training they receive in the company in statistical process control of the software development process. This in turn augments the Japanese approach to continuous process improvement as a means to quality improvement. This coupled with their in-house training has improved their ability to produce software. Again, the reader is cautioned not to infer that all Japanese software is developed under strict statistical process control. While this seems to be the case in the larger organizations, it is not true in general.

In Europe, there is a growing interest in the use of formal methods such as the Vienna Development Method, Z, etc. They clearly provide the mathematical formalism and rigor that is needed as the foundation of software. There is some significant industrial commitment to the use of formal methods. While the impact of formal methods on software development in Europe is unknown, its potential is significant.

From Motorola's benchmarking activities we conclude that there is a need for training in both statistical process control for improvement of the software development process and the introduction of formal methods training as an extension of discrete mathematics for software engineers.

As an interim result of the DACUM analysis and the benchmarking activities, Motorola has developed a preliminary curriculum road map shown in figure 1. The curriculum road map uses the format suggested in our Engineering Training Curriculum System, an internal training planning document used by Motorola. The curriculum consists of developmental and recommended courses based on the following levels: Prerequisites, Entry, Junior/Senior, and Manager. We suggest 144 hours of recommended training for entry level software engineers, 144 hours of recommended training for junior/senior software engineers, and 208 hours of recommended training for software engineering managers. Entry level software engineers are expected to have a BSCS equivalent or CS professional parity. Courses identified with *ENG ???* need to be developed or acquired by Motorola. This curriculum road map requires continuous analysis and refinement.

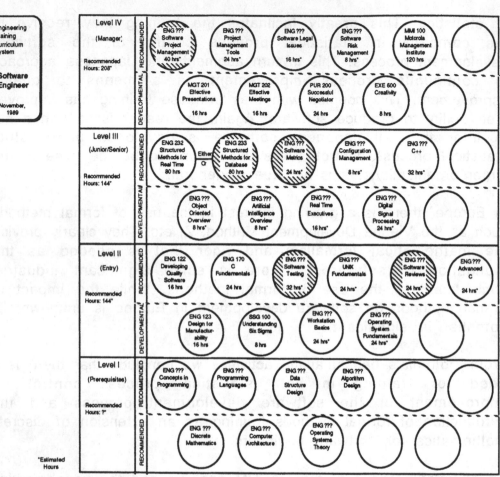

Figure 1

Motorola's software engineering population will require approximately 160,000 man-hours of training per year. This translates to approximately 13,000 man-hours per month. Given an average of twenty students per class and a 24-hour training event (an average of 3 days per class), we estimate that the Motorola software engineering population would require approximately 27 training events per month. Motorola can at best currently satisfy only about one-third of this demand through internal resources.

In addition to the software engineering curriculum road map, Motorola is currently investigating the type and amount of training necessary for engineers to reach computer science parity as an entry point to software engineering. The results of our cooperative efforts with Arizona State University will be used to further this effort.

5. Recent Motorola-University Cooperative Efforts

Motorola and Arizona State University: Motorola's Government Electronics Group and Arizona State University recently cooperated in the transition of electrical engineers into the field of software engineering. This training consisted of twelve weeks of intensive software engineering courses and included a Motorola course on Developing Quality Software, Introduction to Programming and Software Engineering, Data Structures, Introduction to C, Introduction to Computer Architecture, Advanced Ada, Mathematics, and Software Engineering.

Motorola and Tel Aviv University. Motorola Israel does not have an internal software engineering training program. In order to provide the needed training, we have been using Tel Aviv university to provide that training. The focus of this training is languages and tool use. These courses are delivered both at the Motorola facility and the university campus.

Motorola and Florida Atlantic University. Motorola has two major plants in the South Florida area: the Portable Products Division in Plantation and the Paging Division in Boynton Beach. Florida Atlantic University, a near-by educational center, will soon be offering a Masters Degree in Software Engineering based on the Software Engineering Institute's Core Curriculum. The masters degree courses will be offered in Motorola's facilities. In addition, Motorola has provided funds for Apollo Work Stations to be located in Florida State University's Engineering Laboratory.

Motorola and University of Illinois, Chicago. There has been an ongoing relationship between Motorola and U of I, Chicago. The university offers a Master of Science in Computer Science at the Motorola facility.

Nippon Motorola. Nippon Motorola is currently seeking Japanese university faculty who are willing to develop in-house training courses. Their strategy is to base their university relations on future technical requirements

6. Conclusion

This paper represents a snapshot of an ongoing process in Motorola. As such, it is incomplete but represents the process we are using to improve the development and delivery of software engineering training. We have recognized the role that educational institutions can play in software engineering education and training and have described, in part, some of the relationships we have entered into with universities.

Technology Transfer:
The Design, Development, and Implementation of a Process

RebeccaL. Smith
Manager, Technology Transfer Section
Hewlett-Packard Co.
Cupertino, CA

Abstract. *Throughout the past five years, Hewlett-Packard Company's R&D entities in the Networked Systems Sector (Cupertino) have engaged in the systematic implementation of software engineering processes, methods, and tools. The goal: improve software products delivered to HP customers. This effort, led by the Technology Transfer section (TX), has resulted in improvements for several projects in the areas of time-to-market, product quality, and reduced development costs. This paper presents a summary of TX's approach to the design, development, and implementation of a technology transfer process.*

1. Introduction

In 1985 Hewlett-Packard Company chartered its Software Engineering Operation (SEO) in Corporate Engineering to improve HP's software quality and productivity through the acquisition and implementation of management and engineer education programs. The SEO enlightened HP's top executives regarding the necessity and value of a disciplined approach to software engineering, a rapidly evolving field where a computer science graduate becomes technically obsolete only 2 1/2 years after graduating from a 4 year program; furthermore, computer science graduates are often unprepared to immediately begin software engineering.

Putting that management commitment into action within the operating entities became the responsibility of local consulting and education teams such as the Technology Transfer section (TX). To date, HP's software R&D entities in the Networked Systems Sector (NSS; Cupertino) have received the most comprehensive, integrated software engineering processes, methods, and tools program available in the company. This paper provides an overview of the design, development, and implementation of TX's technology transfer process.

2. Evolution of TX

In the Beginning. TX was originally a six-person team within the Quality Department that served one of HP's systems divisions. When the company recognized the need to dedicate resources to the design and development of software engineering tools for its internal systems software developers, the TX team was integrated into a lab that was created to meet that purpose. TX was chartered to develop and implement effective processes for instituting effective software engineering processes, methods, and tools throughout the R&D labs of NSS.

Initially, TX only delivered classes that were developed by SEO. That approach admittedly increased the awareness of a few engineers with regard to generic software engineering methods, but the application of those methods was not systematic. And because no managers were involved in that activity, middle managers had difficulty perceiving the value of a disciplined approach to software engineering.

In a related effort, which also proved counterproductive, many labs chose to install in-house and/or external Computer Aided Software Engineering (CASE) tools in an effort to improve their development processes. Unfortunately, the actual software development processes employed in some of those labs had not been articulated, and the selection of methods was uninformed. Furthermore, the tools that supported specific software engineering methods and processes were not adequately examined prior to their installation. As a result, some of those tools were met with outright rejection, and some managers were discouraged from further considering a non-traditional approach to software development.

1985. In 1985, the standard method of internal technical "training" still involved selecting one or two engineers from a project team and sending them to a class to gain knowledge and skills involving methods, processes, or tools. Those engineers, in turn, would be expected to impart that training to their fellow engineers and managers, a woefully ineffective process.

We in TX readily recognized that if TX was going to generate any real change in the process by which software was developed, we had to work more closely with first and middle-level managers and their teams of engineers. In developing that approach, we began to create programs that addressed the needs of both the managers and their teams, treating them as "intact work groups." Our TX team used a two-prong approach:

1. Empower the R&D teams to properly select and implement software engineering methods.

2. Demonstrate to middle-managers the value, or return on

investment, that resulted from the time they took to implement the software methods and tools.

Over time, this deliberate, systematic integration of software engineering processes, methods, and tools produced tangible results that demonstrated to line managers the value of software engineering. Those results, realized by the few courageous intact work groups of "early adopters", encouraged other managers to consider changing the manner in which their teams perform work.

1985/86. During this period, another factor increased the demand for a coherent, technical education program: the development of Hewlett-Packard's Precision Architecture (HP-PA) Reduced Instruction Set Computing (RISC). HP's move to RISC involved new hardware technologies, new software optimization algorithms, and a host of innovative changes in operating system principles.

TX effectively met the demand for HP-PA engineering knowledge and skills. In collaboration with the people who were creating this technology, we provided thousands of engineers and managers with HP-PA courses that were focused, timely, and effective. That increase in expertise helped Hewlett-Packard to successfully meet the challenge of developing and implementing HP-PA technology. TX responded quickly to the demands of labs who wanted technical knowledge and skills acquisition, thus helping to establish our credibility as a vital link in HP's product development process.

This credibility was accompanied by an expansion of our technology transfer services. Along with classroom training, we began to offer process consulting as well as software engineering tools implementation and on-line support. Managers recognized the expertise available in our team of software engineering consultants, and they began to demand TX services.

1986. TX became entirely self-funded, managed as an internal business.

Today. We continue to generate operating revenue by delivering the myriad TX programs.

3. The TX Model

Because we manage TX as an internal business, we must work closely with our "customers", the R&D management teams. The role of TX has changed, *from* simply delivering technical management and engineering classes, *to* providing organization-focused technology education, accompanied by the essential follow-up consulting for the intact R&D teams. We have evolved into a team of "engineer/consultants", engineers with advanced degrees in computer science and statistics.

As our process evolved for serving engineering labs, we developed a model of our activities. Figure 1 provides a high-level overview of the components of the TX model.

TX's Technology Transfer Model

This model enables us to address the concerns of any lab with whom we work, as reflected in the individual components of the model.

- Engineering Knowledge and Skills: Ensure that the engineers have knowledge and skills in place for effectively developing software.

- Technical Management Knowledge and Skills: Ensure that the managers in that organization have the skills and knowledge they need in order to effectively manage the development of software.

- Engineering Processes, Methods, and Tools: Allow the development team to ensure that 1) they have a clear understanding of what their processes are, 2) they understand what methods are appropriate to use at various phases in the software development life cycle, and 3) they implement the appropriate tools in each instance.

- Software Development Environments: Provide the actual physical configuration for software development, enabling the lab team to effectively implement their software.

- Consulting: Coordinate the transfer, or actual implementation, of the above components of the TX model.

By being able to offer all of those different services to a particular lab, TX helps that lab meet their business objectives. Our integrated approach to education and consulting has enabled product development teams to improve time-to-market, reduce development costs, and improve product quality.

4. Components of TX's Technology Transfer Process

During our process of working with our customers, the TX function must address the unique requirements of several software development labs in Cupertino. To meet this challenge most effectively, the TX staff must continuously evaluate, acquire, and demonstrate essential software engineering expertise. As our team applies this expertise throughout the customer labs, we must also empower those with whom we work to continue to implement effective engineering processes, methods, and tools *after* the consulting process has concluded. While addressing the above, TX treats each customer relationship uniquely, providing our client labs with the optimum design and development processes, methods, and tools for software engineering, enabling them to continuously improve their products.

TX Gets Involved. The technology transfer process is initiated by the first or second-level manager in an R&D lab. Often, that manager has become aware of the need to examine and improve the manner in which the R&D team pursues the tasks of software development. The manager, or managers, involved are also aware of the results that other teams have realized when they changed and improved the process, methods and implemented tools used in their software development work. The team submits a request to TX.

In response, the TX management team assigns an engineer/consultant to work with the R&D team that requested assistance. At the initial stage of this relationship, both parties work together to clarify the R&D managers' reasons, objectives, and expectations that are involved in hiring TX expertise. Our process follows the logical flow diagram shown in Figure 2 (see next page).

As we work with the manager(s) to articulate their business objectives, the TX engineer/consultant assesses the lab's ability to meet those objectives. Following are some of the basic questions that must be answered.

- Does the team possess requisite technical engineering knowledge and skills?

- Can the management team integrate essential project and process management elements into their daily work?

- Is there a clear understanding of the software engineering methods, development environments and supporting tools which will enable the team to

TX's Technology Transfer Process

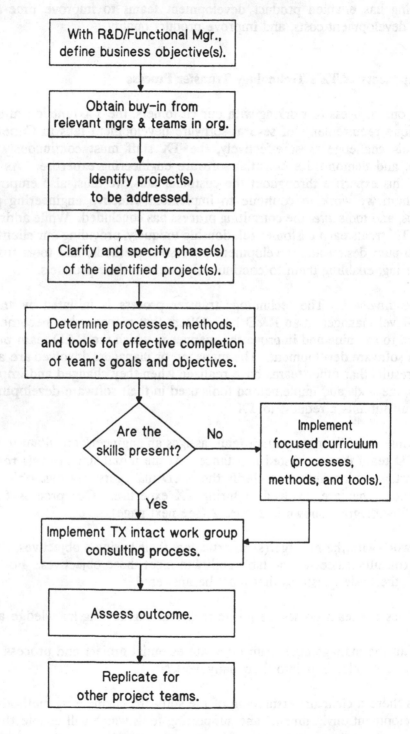

With R&D/Functional Mgr., define business objective(s).

Obtain buy-in from relevant mgrs & teams in org.

Identify project(s) to be addressed.

Clarify and specify phase(s) of the identified project(s).

Determine processes, methods, and tools for effective completion of team's goals and objectives.

Are the skills present?

No → Implement focused curriculum (processes, methods, and tools).

Yes

Implement TX intact work group consulting process.

Assess outcome.

Replicate for other project teams.

Figure 2

meet its business objectives?

The following goals are met as the TX engineer/consultant works with the manager(s) and engineers of the team.

1. Define and improve the software engineering processes, as they are implemented.

2. Ensure that the lab engineers possess critical technical skills.

3. Identify and teach the most appropriate software engineering methods for that team's particular product development phase.

4. Assist the team in its implementation of internal or externally available software engineering tools that support the development process.

5. Delivery Mechanisms

As we move through the steps of the technology transfer process with a lab's management team, TX delivers focused curricula and consulting process plans that enable the lab to most effectively evaluate, change, and improve the manner in which they are developing their software products. We draw on the TX resources shown in Figure 3 (see next page) to create the most effective program for each client lab. By providing an integrated program of the knowledge and skills essential for enabling a lab's ability to meet its business objectives, TX empowers the R&D team to meet those objectives.

Focused Curricula. TX has designed and implemented focused curricula for several lab teams, resulting in the "just-in-time" education critical to maintaining a technically-current engineering work force, with the following results.

- The labs at HP's Cupertino site have ensured that their engineers and managers are up-to-date in the technologies directly affecting their product development work.

- The engineers new to the technologies used in the various labs have demonstrated that their learning curve for essential HP knowledge and skills is much shorter than the traditional mentor/osmosis approach to engineer training.

Graduate Engineer Education. In addition TX has integrated the graduate engineer education courses and degree programs available through Stanford University, the University of California at Berkeley, the California State University at Chico, and the National Technological University. This added learning opportunity helps to

TX's Technology Transfer Resources

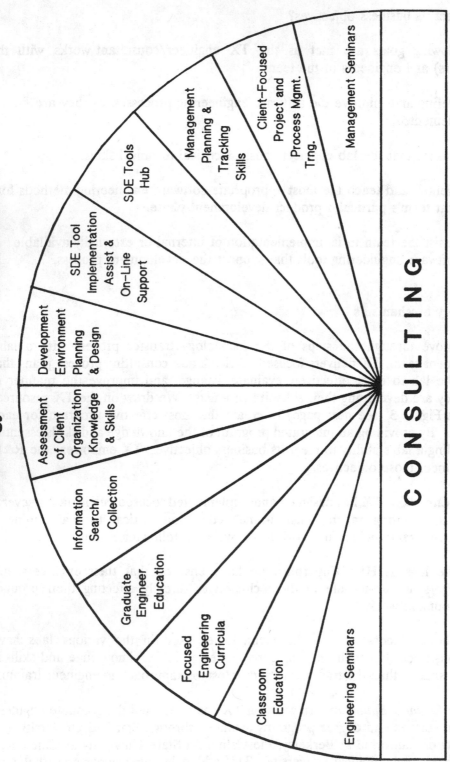

Figure 3

ensure that the Cupertino site engineers are kept technically current. During the past year, more than 14% of the engineers at the Cupertino Site have participated in those university courses.

6. Results

Implementation of the comprehensive and integrated TX model has resulted in significant improvements for several R&D labs as demonstrated in the following examples.

One team reduced the completion time of a product porting process, from 12 weeks, to less than 1 week.

Another team demonstrated that by implementing effective software engineering methods (structured analysis, structured design, and inspections) early in their project, they significantly reduced defects in the final product. The resulting improvement in product quality will mean lower maintenance costs for that lab.

A third team reduced their build time from three days to less than 30 minutes by eliminating the complexity in their process and by implementing a configuration management tool.

7. Conclusion

Significant improvements in HP's software products have resulted from TX's comprehensive and integrated approach to transferring software engineering technologies. Throughout the past five years, TX has demonstrated that *classes alone will not create improvements in software that Hewlett-Packard designs, develops, and delivers to its customers.*

On the contrary, R&D managers must constantly balance several factors as they bring products to market. They must be aware of all the following.

- Customer needs and requirements.

- New technologies and the technical capabilities of their own resources.

- Market windows and other factors that affect product delivery.

- Effective software development environments, processes, methods, and tools.

- Factors that influence the integration of R&D activities with
  the activities of marketing, sales, and support teams.

They must also constantly seek ways to improve their teams' development processes so that their products remain competitive.

TX, as a function, engages in the continuous improvement of our own processes; therefore, we continue to articulate, refine, and integrate effective software engineering principles into our own process as well as in our consulting with HP's software development labs.

By providing consulting and education -- involving software engineering process, methods, and tools -- to R&D teams throughout HP's Cupertino site entities, the TX function has contributed to the company's ability to improve R&D effectiveness, time-to-market, and product quality.

Acknowledgements

As a reflection of the comprehensive and integrated nature of our work in TX, the content and production of this paper represents the efforts of all TX members.

Bibliography

Brooks, F.P., Jr. *No Silver Bullet*. IEEE Computing. 20,4 (Jan. 1987), 10-19.

Gibbs, N.E. *The SEI Education Program: The Challenge of Teaching Future Software Engineers*. Communications of the ACM. 32,5 (May 1989), 594-605.

Humphrey, W.S. *Managing the Software Process*. Addison-Wesley Company, Inc., 1989.

Loh, M. and Nelson, R.R. *Reaping CASE Harvests*. Datamation (July 1, 1989), 31-34.

McWilliams, G. *Integrated Computing Environments*. Datamation (May 1, 1989), 18-21.

Norman, R.J. and Nunamaker, J.F.,Jr. *CASE Productivity Perceptions of Software Engineering Professionals*. Communications of the ACM. 32,9 (Sept. 1989), 1102-1108.

Raghavan, S.A. and Chand, D.R. *Diffusing Software-Engineering Methods*. IEEE Software, (July, 1989), 81-89.

Scacchi, W. *Understanding Software Technology Transfer: Barriers to Innovation Engineering*. IEEE, (TH0218-8/88), 130-135.

Willis, R.R. *Technology Transfer Takes 6 +/- 2 Years*. IEEE, (CH1883-8/83), 108-117.

Zucconi, L. *Selecting a CASE Tool*. ACM SIGSOFT, Software Engineering Notes, 14,2. (Apr 1989), 42-44.

An Undergraduate Curriculum in Software Engineering

H. D. Mills, J. R. Newman, C. B. Engle, Jr.
Florida Institute of Technology

Abstract

Software development and maintenance is only a human generation old, but is already practiced widely in government, business, and university operations on a trial and error, heuristic basis that is typical in such a new human activity. The term software engineering is also widely used as a commercial buzzword for marketing short courses and tools for specific heuristic approaches to software development and maintenance. But legitimate engineering processes, such as found in civil, mechanical, or electrical engineering, have foundations in mathematics and science that require four year university curricula, not three day short courses. Foundations in mathematics and computer science are just reaching the point where legitimate undergraduate engineering curricula are possible for software engineering. Florida Institute of Technology (FIT) plans to develop an undergraduate software engineering curriculum to provide students with new capabilities and standards for software development, evolution, and maintenance.

Software Goes Critical

This 'first generation' of consumers or users have encountered great frustration in dealing with the products of this human activity in software development. With all the people involved, with all the critical uses of software in both commercial and military operations, it is hard to remember that software development is only a human generation old. When civil engineering was a human generation old, the right triangle was yet to be invented. When accounting was a human generation old, double entry was yet to be invented. There are many more people in software in its first generation than there were in civil engineering or accounting in their first generations. But fundamental ideas still take time to discover and develop, and the very number of people in software today creates a massive intellectual inertia to make good use of fundamental ideas as they appear.

Typically, plans and schedules are easy to make for writing the software. The problem is in getting the software to work at all, and to do the right thing when it does work. Software has turned out to be more complex than it first appears. Twenty line programs, even hundred line programs in school problems don't seem hard. But twenty thousand lines of software, let alone a hundred thousand or million lines of software is quite a different matter. First many people will be writing small parts, a few hundred or thousand lines, which may work by themselves quite well. And some such parts may be written years later than others by complete strangers to earlier authors. But these parts must all work together, with no common sense run time help from their authors. That's where the complexity comes in.

So realistic development schedules involves engineering the software to execute in a completely reliable way under all circumstances. There is not enough time to build such software by trial and error. It needs to be engineered, with engineering checks and balances, dictated by an engineering discipline, complete with engineering inspections of work in progress. In fact, such engineering has been demonstrated in large systems in meeting schedules and budgets. For example in both the NASA space shuttle system (over 100 million bytes) and the Navy LAMPS helicopter and ship system (over 10 million words), every delivery over a four year period was on time and under budget [Mills 80]. But human society and institutions have had no long term, orderly experience or expectations in this engineering discipline because of the short time it has been needed.

The Role of Universities in Software Engineering

The current role of universities in software engineering is also in its infancy. During the present human generation, universities have begun to do research in and teach computer science. As a result, many universities now have computer science departments, which may be located in liberal arts, science, or engineering divisions. Such computer science departments teach computer programming and software system development as part of the computer science curriculum, but seldom teach computer programming as an engineering discipline. They seldom teach software maintenance or evolution in a serious way, even though that is what most of their graduates will be asked to do. There are many interesting approaches to teaching computer programming, using graphics, logic, text formats, but it is such a new human activity that there is still much to learn and be sorted out.

The next need is to move from computer science as a base into software engineering, just as more mature engineering disciplines have used sciences and mathematics as their foundations. The 1989 SEI Workshop on an Undergraduate Software Engineering Curriculum [Gibbs 89] pulled together much of the current thinking on the subject. This Workshop sponsored a set of position statements about the needs and pitfalls of putting a software engineering curriculum into place. [Deimel 89] makes the point that computer programming is, indeed, an important part of software engineering, and yet is not treated as seriously as it should be "under the assumption that entering students already know what they need to know about programming."

[Engle 89] discusses the difference between computer science and software engineering, noting that "software for large systems must be developed in a fundamentally different manner than software for small systems." [Ford 89] points out that a software engineering curriculum distinct from computer science is inevitable, but that change is slow and difficult in universities. That change has been difficult already in moving computer science into universities at the expense of established departments.

[Van Scoy 89] describes a specific plan for an undergraduate software engineering curriculum within an existing computer science program. The plan is described in five steps, namely: 1. Change the programming language taught to entering students (to a language which supports software engineering such as Ada); 2. Revise the sequence of courses taken by all freshman and sophomore computer science majors; 3. Add software engineering electives to the computer science major at the junior and senior levels; 4. Split the current computer science major into two tracks; 5. Develop distinct BS CS and BS SE programs. Van Scoy discusses a specific proposal for CS1 [Denning 88] using Ada "to facilitate the teaching of some software engineering ideas subtly and early." This proposal revolves around Ada packages at the outset, first in using packages, second in designing and implementing packages, then finishing with an introduction to Ada tasks. Most of Ada is introduced in the package framework, rather than beginning with procedures and functions before advancing to packages.

[Gibbs 89a] emphasizes the need for computer science fundamentals in undergraduate software engineering, outlining a model curriculum with two years each in Core Computer Science, Mathematics, Software Engineering, and Computer Science. At FIT, our plan is similar in some ways to that discussed in Van Scoy, but even closer to the model curriculum given by Gibbs. As Van Scoy suggests, we plan to evolve a software engineering curriculum within a computer science program. And as Gibbs recommends, we will begin with two years each in Core Computer Science and Mathematics, then finish with two years each in Software Engineering and Computer Science much in the spirit of the Gibbs model curriculum.

As a practical matter, we view Software Engineering as the necessary preparation for the practicing, software development and maintenance professional. The Computer Scientist is preparing for further theoretical studies or specializing in one of the many sub-disciplines such as graphics, artificial intelligence, etc.

Our approach takes its roots in the Denning report [Denning 88]. In addition we have been influenced by the curriculum report on software engineering made by the British Computer Society and Institution of Electrical Engineers [BCS/IEE 89]. Our approach to defining the curriculum for Software engineering is still developing, with our major emphasis at this time being devoted to the first two years.

Starting Right at the Freshman/Sophomore Level

In such a young subject as computer science or software engineering, many topics in graduate school are there because they are recent in origin, not more complex. Certainly our current students should not have to complete an undergraduate degree, spend some time working in the real world encountering the wrong way to create software, then return for a graduate degree before we teach them the right way to do software engineering. For example, we believe that the SEI Report on Graduate Software Engineering Education [Ardis 89] provides a good background for future undergraduate curriculum planning. The material and objectives presented in this report, seems natural to migrate down to the upper undergraduate levels as they become better articulated and agreed upon by the software engineering community. However, we expect to migrate the more formal topics of today's graduate software engineering programs right down to the freshman/sophomore levels.

In fact, the challenge in many science and engineering areas has always been to find simpler rigorous ideas more powerful than early heuristic ideas born out of immediate practice. For example, in mathematics, ordinary arithmetic preceded group theory, then set theory, by hundreds of years. Sets are simple and powerful, but took much human time to discover for effective use. In computer science today, the simple mathematical ideas have also arrived later than the initial practical heuristic ideas about program design. But we believe we can start university students learning the necessary engineering fundamentals to create correct and efficient software. This is possible through the use of mathematical foundations just because those foundations are simple, easily understood mathematical ideas in sets, functions, relations, not even requiring numbers in any necessary way.

We plan to create freshman/sophomore course work to introduce computer programs as mathematical objects from the start, with their expressions and analyses in programming languages as integral parts of the concept. A computer program is a rule for a mathematical function that maps a set of initial states to their final states. This course work is not about writing programs by trial and error. It is about the mathematical derivation of programs as rules for functions from formal specifications, which are mathematical relations or functions themselves.

We plan to make Ada the primary undergraduate curriculum programming language, even though other programming languages will be taught. However, the point of Ada as a programming language is its use to describe rules for mathematical functions that can be analyzed for correctness and performance with mathematical rigor. Other languages, such as assembly languages, Fortran, etc. can also be used to describe rules for these mathematical functions, as well. This shift from viewing programs as step by step instructions to computers (which they certainly are) to a new form of function rules brings mathematical rigor and engineering discipline into direct focus.

Ada as the Base Undergraduate Programming Language

Ada offers many advantages as a base language for the curriculum. It is rich enough to be useful for most programming concepts; it is a practical language, finding widespread acceptance in government, and thus, industry.

Ada is the first programming language which was "engineered" to support software engineering. Ada was not an evolutionary language
where new features were added to an existing shell. Rather, the Ada language was designed as any other software product. This effort was initiated by soliciting and obtaining a series of requirements for the new language. These requirements were refined by widespread public review into a set of specifications upon which a design could be developed. This preliminary design was also given widespread review and a final design for the language was approved, before any implementations of the language existed. This was a novel concept in the design of programming languages; obtain consensus on the requirements before implementing it! This shows that Ada was designed and engineered to perform specific functions, prominent among them was the support of software engineering concepts.

The concepts which Ada was expressly designed to support include abstraction, information hiding, localization, completeness, modularity, reliability, maintainability, reusability, and extendibility, among others. This list gives credence to the claim that the design of Ada was intended to support modern software engineering concepts and practices as we understood them. Arguably, the implementation of the language manifest in numerous compilers on numerous machine configurations, provides the much needed support for software engineering that has been missing in older languages.

The support of modern software engineering practices and concepts is very important. If a language is very rich in expressiveness, then it becomes less difficult and less error prone to translate the problem to be solved from the design space to the solution space. If the language is somewhat limited or constrained in its expressive power, then the mapping from the design space to solution space is more difficult. For example, if the design of a solution to the problem at hand conceptually requires the concept of parallelism, then if the language in which the design is being implemented supports parallelism, this portion of the solution can be directly mapped from the design to the implementation. If, on the other hand, your language does NOT support parallelism, then you must serialize your conceptual parallelism, which means that you must introduce additional complexity into the implementation to achieve the effect of your design. This necessarily perturbs the design and makes maintenance more difficult. In summary, the more powerful the language in terms of expressiveness, the more easily you can map the design to the implementation without introducing additional complexity.

In view of the foregoing, the rich set of constructs and programming expressiveness available in Ada make it the logical choice for our curriculum. While some may argue that the language is "too big" or too complex" for freshmen, we take the opposite view. We need only acquaint the student with that portion of the language which is necessary for them to solve the problems that we provide. In time, this will be the full language. What we obtain from this is the ability to go from simple sequential concepts to more complex ideas such as parallelism or genericity without having to transition the student from a smaller, less powerful language to Ada. They will have been using the same language since the first programming assignment!

Freshman/Sophomore Strategy

At a more general level, we see freshman/sophomore course work dealing with two main areas of core computer science, namely:

    Base Knowledge
        Computer Operations
        Computer Programming Languages
        Data/Text Processing and Storage

    Base Skills
        Program Analysis/Design
        Algorithm Analysis/Design
        Formal Syntax/Semantics Methods
        Data Structures/Access Methods
        Systems Analysis/Design

We regard the Base Skills as mathematics skills in the computer domain, as illustrated above with programs viewed as rules for mathematical functions.

FIT is on a quarter basis. We plan to organize the freshman/sophomore course work in the following sequence:

    Quarter 1
        Program Analysis/Design in Characters/Sequences
        Formal Syntax/Semantics of Sequential Programs

Quarter 2
>   Program Extensions to Integers/Arrays/Records
>   Algorithm Performance Analysis/Design

Quarter 3
>   Program Extensions to Reals/Data Abstractions
>   Formal Syntax/Semantics of Program Modules

Quarter 4
>   Programming Languages/Assembler and High Level
>   Generic Extensions to Programming Languages

Quarter 5
>   Program Extensions to Concurrent Execution
>   Concurrent Algorithm Analysis/Design

Quarter 6
>   Program Extensions to Real Time Systems
>   Real Time Algorithm Analysis/Design

Since the subject contents of these courses do not follow a
traditional grouping, we need to prepare much of the material
ourselves.   The contents of the freshman/sophomore stream of
quarter courses will be organized for convenient use in a stream
of semester courses in other universities.

It may be of interest to compare this sequence of contents with
that of [Van Scoy 89]. Van Scoy plans to introduce most of Ada
in the first semester, certainly packages and tasks, in order
to bring more realism into the course. "A relatively small unit
on tasking is included in the first course in the belief that
students bring to CS1 a view of the world that is essentially
concurrent" [Van Scoy 89]. In the sequence planned above, Ada
packages are not introduced until Quarter 3, Ada tasking until
Quarter 5. Although Ada is the underlying programming language
in both cases, the sequence of development is quite different.
There are certainly many merits to Van Scoy's approach.

Our approach teaches mathematical foundations first, with
programming languages used to express engineering designs based
on mathematical reasoning. Those mathematical foundations take
time to develop and understand. For example, in the FIT plan,
the only data introduced in Quarter 1 is characters and
sequences of characters, but formal syntax, semantics, and
proofs of program correctness are fully developed for this
simple data. Characters and sequences correspond to ruler and
compass constructions in geometry, where mathematical proofs can
be introduced in relatively simple contexts. But characters and
sequences are fully capable of defining any operations possible
in programmed computers, such as sorting, searching, or adding
hundred digit numbers! Once such fundamentals are understood,
integers, arrays, and records are introduced in Quarter 2, reals
and data abstractions (Ada packages) in Quarter 3, in each case
with expanded proof rules to deal with mathematical correctness.

Such an approach for the programming language Pascal appears in [Mills 87], a two semester text that develops formal syntax, semantics, and program correctness in characters and files in the first semester before introducing numbers and other data aggregates.

Freshman/Sophomore Coursework Contents

The new freshman/sophomore coursework at FIT is planned for introduction in 1990/91/92, the freshman coursework in 1990/91, the sophomore coursework in 1991/92.

A new text in two volumes is needed for the mainline material on Base Skills in the freshman/sophomore coursework beginning in 1990/91. Volume I (needed 1990/91) will introduce sequential programs and modules as mathematical objects for engineering analysis and design. Volume II (needed 1991/92) will continue with programming generics, concurrent, and real time programs and modules as mathematical objects for more complex engineering analysis and design.

Volume I will introduce sequential programs and modules as rules for mathematical functions, using the sequential parts of the Ada programming language. Volume II will continue the mathematical treatment of generic, concurrent and real time programs and modules, using the remainder of the Ada programming language. Program analysis and design thereby become mathematics based software engineering with a well defined language of application in Ada.

In more detail, the freshman/sophomore mainline coursework is planned in the following sequence:

Quarter 1

Program Analysis/Design in Characters/Sequences
    Sets, relations, functions, predicates. Programs with boolean and character data and sequential files. Programs as rules for mathematical functions. Structured programs as expressions in an algebra of functions. Program specifications as mathematical relations or functions. Program correctness between a specification relation and a program function. Program design as creating rules for functions to meet specification relations.

Formal Syntax/Semantics of Sequential Programs
    Formal syntax and semantics for structured programs with boolean and character data and sequential files. BNF for context free syntax. Uses of BNF in program specification and design.

Quarter 2

Program Extensions to Integers/Arrays/Records
Extension of scalar data to integers and their use
in program analysis and design. Introduction of
aggregate data in arrays, records and their use in
program analysis and design. All language
extensions in both formal syntax and formal
semantics.

Algorithm Performance Analysis/Design
Analysis and design of algorithm performance in
both time and space requirements as well as
correctness. Understanding and creating high
performance at machine levels as well as
programming language levels.

Quarter 3

Program Extensions to Reals/Data Abstractions
Extension of scalar data to reals and their use in
program analysis and design. Roundoff errors and
algorithm design to contain and minimize problems
of numerical approximation. Introduction of data
abstractions for program modules of procedures and
retained data. Data abstractions as state
machines defined by transition functions with
rules defined by the procedures.

Formal Syntax/Semantics of Program Modules
Formal definitions of modules in both syntax and
semantics as extensions of programs. Extension of
program correctness to module correctness.
Relation to object oriented design/development.

Quarter 4

Programming Languages/Assembler and High Level
General properties and possibilities in assembler
and high level programming languages. Translation
between programming languages. Performance
analyses on constraints of programming languages.

Generic Extensions to Programming Languages
Bases for more general, reusable programs and
modules through use of programming generics and
subsequent automatic development of specific
designs by defining parameters.

Quarter 5

Program Extensions to Concurrent Execution
Addition of concurrency to program and module
design with potential nondeterminism in execution
that converts functional behavior to relational
behavior. Extension of program and module
correctness with relational behavior.

Concurrent Algorithm Analysis/Design
Analysis and design of concurrent algorithm
performance in both time and space requirements as
well as correctness. Understanding and optimizing
concurrent performance at machine levels as well
as programming language levels.

Quarter 6

Program Extensions to Real Time Systems
Addition of real time behavior to program and
module design with potential nondeterminism in
real time execution that converts functional
behavior to relational behavior in time.
Extension of concurrent program and module
correctness to real time behavior.

Real Time Algorithm Analysis/Design
Analysis and design of real time algorithm
performance in both time and space requirements as
well as correctness. Understanding and optimizing
performance in real time at machine levels as well
as programming language levels.

Filling out the Undergraduate Curriculum

In our vision, the upper level coursework for undergraduate
software engineering can be divided into three categories:

Junior/Senior Coursework

Programming Language Translators
Assemblers/Linkers/Loaders
Compilers/Interpreters

Base Systems
Operating Systems
Data Base Systems
Real Time Systems
Network Systems
Graphics Systems

> Advanced Skills
>> Large Scale Systems Maintenance
>> Large Scale Systems Development
>> Statistical Quality Control of Software Production
>> Information Systems
>> Artificial Intelligence
>> Law and Ethics

Our plan is to evolve the Junior/Senior coursework more deliberately, beginning 1992-93, from current offerings in computer science, with a new emphasis on both maintenance and development in large scale systems [Linger 88], statistical quality control [Mills 87a].

We expect to provide software engineering undergraduates with entirely new capabilities and standards in large software systems. These capabilities will stem from disciplined software engineers operating in concert in well disciplined teams with common methods. The mathematical basis in programming from the freshman/sophomore work will lead to new expectations in high performance, zero defect software to system specification. Zero defect software, in contrast with defect prone software expected and condoned in today's widespread heuristic methods, is very possible. For example, the 1980 Census system of reading, assembling, and communicating data from marked Census questionnaires to a central point from twenty geographic locations ran its entire ten months of operation with zero defects. This Census system involving over 25 KLOC of software earned its principal software engineer, Paul Friday, a gold medal, the highest award of the Department of Commerce [Mills 86]. The IBM Wheelwriter typewriter product, using three micro processors and 65 KLOC of software has been used by millions since its introduction in 1984 with zero defect performance [Mills 86].

Implementation at Florida Institute of Technology

The material presented in these six freshman/sophomore courses or 30 quarter hours, replaces what has previously been taught in twelve, traditional three hour courses at the same level. This introductory sequence, includes the fundamental body of knowledge any programmer needs to begin correctly and effectively solving real problems. Thus this becomes not only the introductory sequence for software engineers, but for all computer scientist, information systems specialists and to some degree, computer engineers. During the developmental stages of this program, we will have all of our Computer Science students take this sequence. Beginning in the junior year, the student can, through choosing the appropriate elective courses, specialize in what we call our Software Engineering or Information Systems options.

Although it will take three years for our first group of SE majors to complete our introductory sequence, we have already begun to modify our Junior/Senior courses to strengthen our software engineering emphasis. In addition to our existing courses in operating systems, data bases, compilers, graphics, artificial intelligence, analysis of algorithms, data communications, and ethics, we have added specific courses in large scale systems development, and advanced information systems analysis and design. Beginning in the fall of 1990 our present majors will be able to select a software engineering or information systems option, by choosing the appropriate elective courses from those we already offer. We intend to introduce courses in statistical quality control of software production, real time and distributed systems development and others as we can develop the necessary course material.

Software Engineering Techniques for Non-Computer Science Majors

If, as we project, this is the proper way to train software engineers to correctly solve problems using the available computing resources, it is also necessary to address the needs of other academic disciplines to introduce their scientists, engineers, businessmen etc. to these new techniques. We accept the premise that in developing large scale computer based systems, a team of specialists will be involved. In this environment it is reasonable to expect a greater depth of knowledge of the software engineering techniques by the software specialists. We recognize, however, that as problem solving using computers continues to pervade every academic discipline, we have an obligation to distill the essence of software engineering into a sequence of service courses for other disciplines. It is our plan to develop such a series of service courses based on our experience with our Freshman/Sophomore sequence.

Conclusions

The Computer Science Department at the Florida Institute of Technology will incrementally introduce a software engineering undergraduate degree, beginning in the fall of 1990. The curriculum will emphasize mathematical derivation of programs from formal specifications, which are mathematical objects themselves. From this formal basis the analysis, design and implementation of systems, programs and component modules will be developed. Ada will be used as the common basis because of its valuable properties and future widespread use. Upon this formal foundation, topics in software architecture, computer systems, software analysis and development/maintenance process techniques will be covered. Optional courses will be available at the Junior/Senior level to allow specialization. We will investigate the possibility of condensing the initial two year sequence to serve as service courses to other academic disciplines.

Once we have established the value and creditability of our Software Engineering program and have demonstrated the value of our service courses to other disciplines, we plan to address the issue of accrediting software engineering as a legitimate field in the engineering professions.

In summary, we expect future FIT software engineering graduates to be capable of engineering zero defect software at high productivity, and, of course, to schedules and budgets as well. Such engineering performance requires effective management of a rigorous software engineering process, not simply hoping for the best from heuristics and good intentions.

References

[Ardis 89] M. Ardis and G. Ford, "SEI Report on Graduate Software Engineering Education", in [Gibbs 89], pp 208-250

[BCS/IEE 89] The British Computer Society and The Institution of Electrical Engineers, "A Report on Undergraduate Curricula for Software Engineering", June 1989

[Deimel 89] L. E. Deimel, "Programming and its Relation to Computer Science Education and Software Engineering Education", in [Gibbs 89], pp 253-256

[Denning 88] P. J. Denning, D. E. Comer, D. Gries, M. C. Mulder, A. Tucker, A. J. Turner, and P. R. Young, "Computing as a Discipline: Final Report of the ACM Task Force on the Core of Computer Science", ACM Press 1988

[Engle 89] C. B. Engle, Jr., "Software Engineering is not Computer Science", in [Gibbs 89], pp 257-262

[Ford 89] G. Ford, "Anticipating the Evolution of Undergraduate Software Engineering Curricula", in [Gibbs 89], pp 263-266

[Gibbs 89] N. E. Gibbs (Ed.), Software Engineering Education, Lecture Notes in Computer Science, Springer-Verlag 1989

[Gibbs 89a] N. E. Gibbs, "Is the Time Right for an Undergraduate Software Engineering Degree?", in [Gibbs 89], pp 271-274

[Linger 88] R. C. Linger and H. D. Mills, A Case Study in Cleanroom Software Engineering: The IBM COBOL Structuring Facility, IEEE Compsac 1988

[Mills 80] H. D. Mills, D. O'Neill, R. C. Linger, M. Dyer, R. E. Quinnan, "The Management of Software Engineering", IBM Systems Journal, V 19, 1980

[Mills 86] H. D. Mills, "Structured Programming: Retrospect and Prospect", IEEE Software, November 1986

[Mills 87] H. D. Mills, V. R. Basili, J. D. Gannon, R. G. Hamlet, Principles of Computer Programming: A Mathematical Approach, Wm. C. Brown, 1987

[Mills 87a] H. D. Mills, M. Dyer, and R. C. Linger, "Cleanroom Software Engineering". IEEE Software, September 1987

[Van Scoy 89] F. L. Van Scoy, "Developing an Undergraduate Software Engineering Curriculum within an Existing Computer Science Program", in [Gibbs 89], pp 294-303

[Washington Roundup 1989] Aviation Week and Space Technology, February 6, 1989, p 17

An Undergraduate Programme in Software Engineering

M. F. Bott
Department of Computer Science,
University College of Wales,
Penglais, Aberystwyth,
Dyfed SY23 3BZ, UK

Abstract. *The paper describes an undergraduate curriculum in software engineering which has been developed in close consultation with the software industry. The UK context of such a programme is described and compared to the position in the USA. The programme is noteworthy for its emphasis on design, the use of Ada as the main programming language, and the emphasis on quality.*

1 Background

1.1 UCW Aberystwyth

The University College of Wales, Aberystwyth (UCW) is the oldest of the six constituent colleges of the University of Wales. The structure of the University is comparable to that of multi-campus state universities in the USA. Aberystwyth is a small and isolated town on the coast, some two hours drive from the nearest centres of industry and population, and much further from the main centres of the IT industry. The main industries of the surrounding area are agriculture and tourism.

UCW has about 3000 students; almost all of them are full time and almost all of them have their homes elsewhere.

1.2 Students' Previous Experience

Students come into the programme with a very wide range of computing experience and education. The typical entrant is an 18 year old with two years of calculus, algebra, trigonometry and statistics in high school, as well as probably two years of physics; in addition, he or she probably has some experience of using a microcomputer and of programming, usually in Basic but possibly in Pascal.

However, it would be undesirable to restrict entry to students with this background and many come into the programme with no computing experience at all and with no physics and only basic arithmetic and algebra. At the other extreme, some enter with considerable programming experience in several high level languages and in assembler.

A very important constraint in the design of the programme, therefore, is that it should be accessible to those with no relevant background while presenting a worthwhile challenge to those with extensive relevant experience.

1.3 Degree Programmes in England and Wales

The pattern of undergraduate degree programmes in England and Wales[1] is very different from that in the USA or continental Europe. Although there is some provision for part time studies, the overwhelming majority of students complete their bachelor's degree in three full time years in college, possibly interspersed with periods of industrial training.

Students have much less freedom over their choice of courses than in the USA and spend a much larger proportion of their time studying their main subject. At UCW, a Software Engineering[2] student will spend one third of the first year studying Software Engineering, two thirds of the second year and the whole of the third year; a further third of the first year is spent studying Mathematics and the choices available for the other non-Software Engineering portions of the programme are comparatively limited. Within the Computer Science component, it is only in the final year that students have any real choice over the courses they study. In other universities, it is common to find that there is no choice of subjects at all, outside the main degree programme.

While it can certainly be argued that courses based on this pattern are undesirably narrow, it does mean that the level of knowledge and attainment in the major subject is likely to be perceptibly higher than in a broader course. Very roughly, a student on the Bachelor's programme at UCW will spend the equivalent of 72 credit hours studying Software Engineering and a further 36 studying allied topics such as Mathematics, Microelectronics and Accounting. Because of the level of the Bachelor's degree, employers attach comparatively little value to a Master's degree.

1.4 Validation of Degrees

There are two main ways in which degrees in the UK are validated: by the use of external examiners and by accreditation by professional bodies.

---

[1]Scotland is rather different in this respect.

[2]Although the programme is designed as a Software Engineering programme, for marketing reasons it is still designated as a BSc in Computer Science. For cultural reasons, many British students have been reluctant to embark on courses whose title includes the word 'engineering' but it is hoped that this attitude is changing.

The use of external examiners is universal and applies in all disciplines. Normal practice is that students are examined at the end of the academic year on all the courses that they have taken during the year. A senior academic in the same discipline from another university is invited to participate in examinations for students at the end of their final year with the specific responsibility of ensuring that the standards are comparable with those in his or her own university.

Accreditation by professional bodies is confined to vocational disciplines (Accounting, the various branches of Engineering, Architecture, etc.). The department prepares a written submission describing the programme and the department, including detailed syllabuses, past examination papers, details of equipment, and so on. If this is satisfactory, a group of senior members of the professional body visits the department to inspect its facilities and discuss the programme with staff and students. If all is well, the programme is accredited for a period, typically, of five years. This means that the professional body will accept graduates from the program as having satisfied some part, or possibly all, of the educational requirements required to become a full member. The British Computer Society has accepted the UCW programme as fulfilling all its educational requirements for full membership.

A fuller description of the accreditation process is given in [2].

2 Programme Objectives

The primary objective of the programme is to produce graduates who

- have a professional understanding of the principles of software engineering and can take their place easily and quickly in the software industry and make rapid career progress within the limits of their abilities;

- are competent to use modern software tools and design techniques in their work;

- have a sufficiently broad knowledge of computing topics (theoretical, practical and application oriented) to be able to work anywhere in the software industry, together with a deep knowledge of some areas so as to appreciate how hard problems can be tackled.

We can break down the above objectives to show what we aim to achieve in each year, as follows:

- By the end of the first year, students should know how to design and write well structured, easily maintainable and robust programs to carry out fairly simple tasks reasonably efficiently. They should be fluent in a fairly large subset of the programming language used. They should be competent to use the standard tools (editors, compilers, debuggers) available in the environment in which they have worked. They should understand the importance of testing and have demonstrated the ability to plan and perform it satisfactorily in their work. They should be capable of producing user documentation, design documentation and maintenance documentation for the programs they have written and should understand the importance of this. They should understand, at a fairly superficial level, how processors and the common peripherals work. They should have acquired the necessary mathematical background. Above all, they should understand what distinguishes the professional software engineer from the amateur programmer.

- By the end of the second year, all students should understand the problems of constructing software systems (as opposed to single programs); they should be familiar with a wider range of software tools. They should be able to appreciate systems as a whole and understand the roles of the software and hardware components. They should be competent to handle at a simple level the conventional managerial and quality assurance techniques used for such systems and they should be familiar with a range of modern design techniques. They should be familiar with the problems of real time systems. They should have an appreciation of the role of formalisation in the design and specification process.

- At the end of the third year, students should have demonstrated their ability to carry out the design and implementation of a complete system with full documentation. All students will have studied a range of advanced topics in some depth, including some theoretical topics. They should understand the importance of theory as the basis for designing robust and reliable systems. They should have a sound understanding of the responsibilities and obligations of the professional engineer.

3   Relationships with Industry

The geographical remoteness of Aberystwyth makes for some difficulty in setting up relationships with industry and some modes of cooperation are clearly impossible. There was always a danger that physical remoteness would be equated with technical irrelevance and so, to avoid this, we were forced early into closer partnership with industry than was common at that time in the UK. The initial impetus came from several faculty members who had substantial experience at a senior level in the software industry and were keen to maintain their contacts.

The Department has two strong research groups, in Software Engineering and in Robotics, and all the research work is done in collaboration with industry. This brings visiting industrialists to the Department on a regular basis and gives the opportunity to discuss curriculum issues and other topics, as well as the joint research work.

The Department runs a series of weekly lectures by outside speakers, the majority of whom are from industry. Final year students are expected to attend these lectures and the material is regarded as examinable.

Students are strongly encouraged to spend a year working in the software industry, between their second and third years in College, and some 50% of them do so. We have no difficulty in finding placements; indeed, we are frequently embarrassed by our inability to fill all the places offered. Students are placed in a very wide variety of organisations, from orthodox data processing shops to 'leading edge' software houses and hardware suppliers. Besides the very considerable benefits to the students themselves, the visits which members of staff make to the students and their employers during this period are a source of valuable feedback to the Department. The variety of the placements makes this feedback especially valuable because we meet organisations with which our research work would otherwise give us little contact.

4 The Choice of Programming Language

Over the years we had become increasingly dissatisfied with Pascal as a vehicle for demonstrating and practising the principles of software engineering. The major weaknesses were felt to be the lack of support for information hiding, separate compilation and concurrency, together with the difficulty of interfacing with UNIX facilities such as *curses*. These weaknesses were felt particularly acutely in group project work. We were also aware of a lack of support tools, notwithstanding the excellence of the Berkeley compiler; we felt we would want to make increasing use of such tools in our future teaching and that there was little prospect of their becoming available.

The replacement for Pascal had to be a language which was well supported and of whose longevity we could be certain — the effort and upheaval involved in changing the main teaching language is substantial and we had no wish to repeat the process for a very long time. The only candidates which met these requirements and which remedied the perceived weaknesses in Pascal were Ada and Modula-2. Of the two, Ada was preferred because:

- it meets the technical requirements more comprehensively;

- the level of support is already better than for Modula-2 and is improving;

- the level of investment in the language guarantees its continued existence and importance;

- it is more vocationally relevant.

More detail about our experiences in using Ada as a first teaching language is given in [1].

In order to provide a contrast with imperative programming languages, a functional language (ML) is taught as part of the second year course.

5 The First Year Course

In common with other institutions, we have suffered in recent years from the wide variations in computing background to be found amongst our first year undergraduates; some have done two or three years of Computing in high school, some have been enthusiastic hobbyists and some have never touched a keyboard. In order to accommodate the needs of such a diverse collection of students, and because it seemed right in the context of the course as a whole, we had already developed a first year module with a strong emphasis on program design. Students do not start coding until quite late in the first term.

The use of the computing facilities is taught separately from the programming, largely in supervised laboratory classes, and beginners get supplementary teaching to bring them up to the necessary level of competence.

Ada fits very well into this framework. Students are first introduced to the package as the fundamental building block for programs expressed in Ada; the program library is then introduced, followed by the subprogram as the basic executable unit. Only after this are students introduced to the lower level statements of the language.

The subset of the language taught in the first year is conditioned by the general approach adopted. Some supposedly advanced topics such as private types, limited private types and generics are taught because they are fundamental to the ideas of abstraction, information hiding and data encapsulation; exception handling is taught because it is essential for the construction of robust programs. Other features of the language are left to be taught in second year units at the point where the need for them becomes apparent; the obvious example is tasking, which is taught during the treatment of concurrency in the Operating Systems unit.

6 The Second Year

The second year contains much material which will be found in conventional Computer Science programmes; rather than describing this, we shall concentrate on some of the more unusual features of this part of the course.

6.1 Design Methodologies

We do not feel it is desirable — nor, indeed, practicable — to teach a complete design methodology in all its aspects. Nevertheless, students should be sufficiently aware of such methodologies to understand their value and their limitations. We therefore teach two contrasting methodologies to a level that allows students to to carry out the basic design steps of the method; to use and understand its notations; and to understand the design paradigm which underlies it.

The methodologies taught are SSADM [5], for the design of information systems, and MASCOT [7], for designing real time embedded systems. Both methodologies are UK government standards for their respective areas of application. They are taught within courses which cover these areas.

6.2 The Group Project

A group project forms a major part of the second year course and constitutes one twelfth of the total assessment for the year's work.

Students work in groups of six, with a faculty member playing the role of 'client' and also acting as an informal consultant. Each group starts from a very brief statement of requirements; the following is a typical example:

> A test data generator is required which will accept a record specification made up of field descriptors and generate random records matching the specification. As well as the usual field types (alpha, numeric, etc.), it must be possible to generate fields containing plausible names and addresses.

In consultation with the client, the group is expected first to develop a detailed requirements specification and then continue through to implementation, system testing and acceptance testing by the client. They are expected to produce the following deliverables, on dates agreed with the client:

- quality plan;
- requirements specification;
- design specification;
- test plan;
- user documentation;
- maintenance documentation;
- code listings and test results.

In addition, they are expected to use orthodox project planning and monitoring techniques; the quality plan must include procedures for configuration management, design reviews and code walkthroughs.

The major difficulty we have faced in running group projects is that the dynamics of the group have led to group members spending far too much time on the project, to the detriment of their other work. We have been able to keep this problem under control in three ways:

- careful selection of projects, to ensure that they are not too large, too difficult or too interesting;
- advising students that no more than 80 hours should be spent on the project and requiring them to keep and submit diaries of their work;
- judicious advice from the client.

Group projects were introduced into the course some six years ago and have proved universally popular with our industrial advisers and with the employers of our students. A substantial majority of the students also reacts very positively to the experience but there are always a few students who do not succeed in coming to terms with group working within the time available.

Associated with the group project, there is a conventionally taught course covering the software life cycle, with particular emphasis on quality, management and design.

6.3 Hardware Teaching

We believe that all software engineers should have a sufficient understanding of hardware to be able to communicate with hardware engineers where their work must interface. The first year course covers the basics of processor design and common peripherals, at the logical level. In the second year students take a very practical course intended to give them an appreciation of the way in which hardware influences overall system performance and, in particular, the implications for performance of different hardware strategies and architectures. Students are not assumed to have any background in Electronics, or even Physics, before entering the course.

This course is described in more detail in [6].

7 The Third Year

A major component of the third year course is an individual project which accounts for one quarter of the third year assessment. The purpose of the project is to allow students to demonstrate their ability to specify, design, construct, test and document a complete and non-trivial piece of software. We discourage projects which involve too large an element of research, on the grounds that the research component would tend to drive out the engineering content.

Students in their third year are required to take a course entitled 'Professional Issues in Software Engineering'. This covers material on finance and management, on legal issues (product liability, data protection, intellectual property rights), health and safety issues and labour relations. The material on finance and management is taught by faculty members from Computer Science, on the basis of their own experience in the industry; we are fortunate that other departments are able to provide staff with relevant, non-academic experience to teach the remaining topics.

8 Evaluation

8.1 Education versus Training

A satisfactory balance between education and training in a vocational programme is notoriously difficult to achieve. The programme described here is clearly open to the criticism that there is too much training in the use of current tools and techniques and insufficient coverage of fundamental concepts and current research directions. Such a criticism is all the more likely to be levelled at the programme in the UK, where graduate students normally embark on a PhD programme immediately after completing their Bachelor's degree.

In response to this criticism, we would offer the following rejoinders:

- We take care to include a variety of tools and techniques sufficient to ensure that students are flexible enough to adapt to ones they haven't yet met. Someone whose only experience of programming is in an imperative language may well have difficulty in adapting to a different programming paradigm but someone with experience of both the imperative and functional paradigms is unlikely to have much difficulty in the face of a third paradigm, and similarly for design methodologies. Furthermore, students are strongly encouraged to think carefully about the differences between the techniques they are learning and between the underlying assumptions.

- The average student finds it much easier to understand abstractions when they derive from concrete experience; such concrete experience can only be gained by using concrete tools and techniques.

- As with any undergraduate programme, comparatively few students go on to a PhD. The main customer for our students is the software industry and all the feedback we receive suggests that it is well satisfied with our approach. To orient the course towards producing PhD students would be to allow the tail to wag the dog. In any case, there are plenty of opportunities for potential PhD students to deepen their knowledge and demonstrate their potential through the project work.

8.2 Teaching Design

We are under no illusions about the difficulty of teaching design. Our approach contains four elements;

- make students understand the importance of design by insisting that all practical work they submit includes design as well as implementation;

- constructive criticism of the design work carried out by students;

- teach a number of different design notations and techniques;

- expose students to examples of good and bad design, emphasising the design alternatives and the reasons for the choices made.

We are currently succeeding reasonably well with the first three but there is scope for improving and extending the exposure of students to design examples. The difficulty here is time; serious case studies require much time to be devoted to explaining the context in which the design work was carried out.

8.3 Ada

There is a myth that Ada is too large and complex a language to be taught satisfactorily to beginners and that it requires too many resources to be used as the main programming language for an undergraduate programme. Our experience is that these are, indeed, myths. Cobol and PL/I are both more complex languages than Ada and all have been used comparatively successfully for undergraduate teaching. We have found that using Ada as the implementation vehicle when teaching software design has suddenly made the whole process a great deal easier. No longer do we have problems because of the 'structure clashes' between the principles which we want to teach and the limitations of the implementation language. This is perhaps best seen by considering information hiding and software reuse; Pascal provides no useful support for either of these — quite the contrary, indeed — while Ada provides, at least at undergraduate level, more or less exactly what is needed.

9 Future Developments

A major priority in the development of the programme is to increase the range of software tools available to the students, particularly in the area of design. The rapid evolution of CASE tools in the last few years has made it difficult to select a stable and useful set for instructional purposes but it is essential that we do this.

We are conscious of the fact that the programme gives little attention to issues of software maintenance. This is certainly a weakness that we wish to remedy; a possible approach is described in [3]. However, this — and a number of other areas that we would like to expand — raises the problem of space within the programme.

In order to tackle these problems, a complete restructuring of the programme is taking place, somewhat along along the lines described in [4]. The major changes in the new programme will be:

- compulsory material on IC design;

- a compulsory (rather than optional) industrial year;

- increased coverage of commercial and legal issues;

- material specifically aimed at safety critical systems;

- greater efforts to improve students' presentational skills, both written and oral.

Students will lose the freedom to choose one third of their second year course from outside the programme. The main programme will be a four year programme and students will be encouraged to undertake this; however, a three year, more limited programme will also be available.

References

[1] M. F. Bott. Experiences with Ada as a first teaching language. *Ada User*, 9(Supplement), 1988.

[2] D. E. Conway, S. C. Dunn, and G. S. Hooper. BCS and IEE accreditation of software engineering courses. *Software Engineering Journal*, 4(4), 1989.

[3] B. J. Cornelius, M. Munro, and D. J. Robson. An approach to software maintenance education. *Software Engineering Journal*, 4(4), 1989.

[4] M. M. Lehman. The Software Engineering first degree at Imperial College, London. In N. E. Gibbs and R. E. Fairley, editors, *Software Engineering Education*. Springer Verlag, 1987.

[5] G. Longworth and D. Nicholls. *SSADM Manual Version 3*. National Computing Centre, Manchester, 1986.

[6] J. J. Rowland. A practical approach to hardware empathy for software engineering students. *Software Engineering Journal*, 4(4), 1989.

[7] H. Simpson. The MASCOT method. *Software Engineering Journal*, 1(3):103–120, 1986.

AN UNDERGRADUATE SOFTWARE ENGINEERING MAJOR

EMBEDDED IN A

COMPUTER SYSTEMS ENGINEERING DEGREE

by K. Reed, MSc, FACS, MIE(Aust) and T. S. Dillon, PhD, FIE(Aust), SMIEEE

Department of Computer Science
La Trobe University
Bundoora, Melbourne 3001
Victoria
Australia

ABSTRACT

This paper describes an undergraduate major stream in Software Engineering embedded in a four year Bachelor of Computer Systems Engineering Degree. This major allows students to specialize in Software Engineering in their third and fourth years, with the result that some 60% of their time is dedicated to Computer Science and Software Engineering.

This contrasts with the post graduate Master's programs offered in the US, and the relatively minor Software Engineering subjects offered in some undergraduate Computer Science courses.

1. INTRODUCTION

The fact that traditional engineering concepts can be applied to software production is finally being widely recognized. It is now accepted that Software Engineering, a practicable discipline similar in form to other established engineering disciplines, can be considered to have come of age.

At the same time, the need for formal education for software engineers is becoming generally accepted, although there are relatively few degree courses with dedicated to this subject. The need for specialized courses in Software Engineering arose from the widely held belief that conventional Computer Science and Business EDP degrees do not really concentrate on producing practitioners capable of building reliable software to a given specification and to some predetermined schedule [GIB89a] Specifically tailored programs were first introduced about ten years ago, and were based on Master's degrees by course work [FRE87], [KEE81] following a series of curriculum proposals by ACM [FAI87]. Today, some twenty years after the original NATO Conferences on Software Engineering, serious consideration is only just being given to the introduction of undergraduate Software Engineering degrees.

Interestingly enough, similar arguments can be applied to Digital Computer Engineering, and to Computer Network Engineering, bodies of knowledge which are currently (in Australia at least) taught as minor elements of either Computer Science or Electronic Engineering degrees.

Recent studies in Australia have provided evidence of a chronic shortage in each of the above areas. This prompted the Department of Computer Science at La Trobe University in Melbourne Australia, to develop a four year undergraduate Computer Systems Engineering Degree, with majors in Software Engineering, Digital Computer Engineering and Computer Network Engineering.

This paper concentrates upon the Software Engineering major, however, the the other two majors provide students with an opportunity to acquire a specialized qualification in courses especially constructed for that purpose, something which is rare in this country at least.

We begin by summarizing the current state of Software Engineering education, and relate that to both Digital Computer and Computer Network Engineering. We then provide an outline of the complete degree structure, and continue by dealing with the difference between Software Engineering and Computer Science as seen by educators. We conclude with a detailed description of the Software Engineering major, summarizing the syllabi, and relating them to the existing undergraduate Computer Science offerings.

2. THE COMPUTER SYSTEMS ENGINEERING DEGREE

2.1. Motivation

Software Engineering education currently falls into approximately two categories:

a)   Master's by course work degrees dedicated to the subject, such as those pioneered by Seattle University [LEE81] and the Wang Institute ([ARD87] and [ARD85], and [MCK87].

b)   A cursory outline of Software Engineering, usually concentrating on project management and systems analysis, and incorporating a team subject. This would usually be taught as a final year component in an undergraduate Computer Science degree.

Both of these approaches are unsatisfactory, although the underlying reasons for their existence are understandable. The English tradition of "liberal arts" education which has been adopted in the United States and many other countries (including Australia) means that the total amount of teaching hours available for vocationally oriented material is limited. The time available for specialist subjects which could legitimately be included in a Computer Science major is therefore restricted, preventing additional space from being made available for Software Engineering.

There has also been a strong view, particularly in the United States that software engineering should be only taught to people who already have an undergraduate qualification and significant industrial experience (see [GIB89A] p272). Increasingly however, the view is being taken that this approach is unsatisfactory because it smacks of locking the stable door after the horse has bolted.

An alternate view is that proper software engineering habits should be learnt at the outset of one's career as a software producer. This is to be preferred to the current approach of trying to correct a lengthy period of inappropriate practices which were acquired during basic undergraduate training with the full authority of academic staff. Fortunately, the last few years have seen a gradual increase in the undergraduate emphasis on Software Engineering, however, the current situation still leaves a lot to be desired.

A slightly different problem exists with respect to computer systems engineering, an area, which, in recent times, has seen a rash of offerings in Computer Engineering. These have frequently been mounted by Electronic Engineering Departments and sometimes consist of little more than the study of the application of microprocessors in embedded computer systems for process control or real time applications.

The reality is that computer engineering or computer systems engineering is in fact a much broader discipline requiring a proper understanding of the engineering of an entire computer system. A detailed knowledge of computer architecture, computer communication systems, software systems and lastly of multi-processor computer systems must be acquired before one can be considered a Digital Computer Engineer.

Recognition of this fact is leading to a reappraisal of the notion of computer systems engineering as is illustrated by the recent move of Computer Engineering from the Electronic Engineering Department to the Department of Computer Science and Engineering at the University of Washington. Recognition that Digital Computer Engineering is a discipline in its own right, much in the manner of Civil Engineering, Mechanical Engineering, Electrical or Electronic Engineering, rather than a sub-branch of Electronic Engineering is likely to grow. At the same time, practitioners and educators are becoming increasingly aware that the the principles underlying this discipline are somewhat different from those that underly the enabling technologies of microelectronics and digital design.

Similar remarks apply to Computer Network Engineering.

The authors' view is that all three bodies of knowledge have matured to a point where they can be regarded as a set of related but separate disciplines.

This had led the Department of Computer Science at La Trobe University to develop a four year undergraduate degree in Engineering providing for major studies in each of the above disciplines. This paper will provide an outline of the degree but will focus on the Software Engineering component in some detail.

2.2. Aims of the Course

The aims and objectives of the course are to produce qualified professional personnel in the fields of:

1. Software Engineering

2. Computer Architecture and Systems

3. Computer Networks

These personnel should be capable of participating effectively in the design, construction and management of each of the relevant systems. The best graduates should also be well equipped to carry out research in each of the above areas. The course has, however, been designed to be vocational in intent and has been designated as an engineering rather than a science course.

We have chosen this approach since we believe that science is essentially concerned with the understanding of the phenomena under study and the development of new knowledge, whether these phenomena are natural or manmade.

Engineering on the other hand is distinguished by the need not only for an understanding or an analysis of systems but also a strong emphasis on synthesis, and design and construction of systems. It is felt that these processes play a primary role in engineering activities, and that they are best taught within the context of an engineering framework. Amongst other things, it is our belief that recognition of the above has a significant impact on the practical work prescribed as well as the choices that are made with respect to course content.

In the latter context we regard traditional Computer Science and Electronics as enabling technologies which have the same relationship to Software Engineering, Digital Computer Engineering and Network Engineering as do Physics and Mathematics to Mechanical and Civil Engineering and Chemistry to Chemical Engineering. In particular there is, in Software Engineering, a body of experimental evidence which suggests that the natural problem solving processes used by programmers and system developers require a substantial knowledge of a large number of basic concepts and techniques. This is a matter which we have attempted to address in this course.

2.3. Course Structure

The first two years of the Degree are common to all streams with students being able to select one or the three major streams after the third and fourth year. Common core material is necessary in the basic sciences and Mathematics, and in the enabling technologies of Computer Science and Electronics. This is included in the first two years. (See figure 1 below).

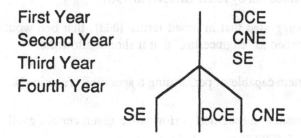

Figure 1. BCSE Degree Structure

Specialization in the principles of Computer Systems Engineering begins in the second year. This reflects our view that Computer Systems Engineers should, irrespective of chosen specialization, be well educated in the basic technologies and the basic sciences concerned. In the third year there is an opportunity to specialize in each of the three streams, while still taking some units from the other two. For example Digital Computer Engineering majors will undertake more computer architecture and related material than related Software Engineering majors. Software Engineering majors will focus very heavily on their chosen filed, while still taking some material in relation to computer architecture and networks. This specialization increases considerably in the fourth year of the course, and allows the individual disciplines to be given adequate weight, a situation that is not possible in traditional educational systems.

There is an emphasis throughout the course in understanding both the software and hardware implication of each of the major streams.

The belief that an engineering education should involve a strong theme of "learning by doing" is reflected in a strong component of practical work in each of the second, third and fourth years. This is achieved through the medium of laboratory classes which are closely supervised, whilst a considerable component is in the form of project work. The emphasis in Software Engineering will be on the acquisition of practical experience in applying techniques in second and third year within the framework of group projects. A major team project in fourth year would be conducted in a simulated software house environment, Horning's famous "software hut" [HOR77].

3. SOFTWARE ENGINEERING AND COMPUTER SCIENCE EDUCATION

3.1. What is Software Engineering?

Software Engineering is the result of bringing traditional engineering discipline to bear on the process of building software systems. Software Engineering is a discipline dependent on a number of technologies. It uses **managerial techniques** to control and manage projects, **systems analysis** techniques to capture a series of descriptions of a system that is capable of being converted, by **programming**, into a machine executable form, as has been pointed out by Reed [REE87] in 1987.

It was further suggested that in broad terms [ibid], that one would expect, for any discipline to be described as "engineering" that it should allow the:

a)   Design of a system capable of performing a specified "function".

b)   Design of a system to a specified performance given certain available run-time and implementation resources.

c)   Implemention of a system to a required time-cost schedule.

d)   Maintainence and enhancement of the system during its life.

These goals can be achieved through...

A)   Component re-use, both code, module and design,

C)   Tool use, to control and lend power to the process of system description, code production, testing and quality control,

C)   Design iteration, to meet both performance and functional goals,

and

D) Management techniques to describe the system development process, estimate resource requirements, and monitor resource usage.

The above constitutes an extension of the definitions given in Richard Fairley's book [FAI85] in that we explicitly recognize the element of performance as a possible design criteria, and add the design iteration requirement. Interestingly enough, otherwise excellent Software Engineering textbooks do not attempt a compact definition of the field. See for example Pressman [PRE88].

These goals cannot be met without a large number of techniques and methodologies many of which we currently associate with Systems Analysis and Design [HAW88] and with programming.

Requirements b) & c) cannot be achieved without iteration in the design process, since both the system performance and implementation cost will depend upon aspects of the design.

It should be kept in mind that requirements b) & c) are the keys to effective software projects and products - without them we produce system that will not run on available hardware. The fact is that run-time resource utilization, performance and implementation are affected by the design itself, making design iteration and perhaps prototyping essential. (We should point out that design iteration may also be necessary to determine the functionality of a system cf. prototyping etc. [CAR83]).

It is possible to consider an engineering design process to be one in which a set of parameters are successively altered until a set of target relationships between all of them is obtained, while another set of relationships (constraints), is maintained. The design process may include back-tracking as well as iteration [REE87].

3.2. The Educational Implications of Two Differing Disciplines

Computer Science has as its goal the systematic development of knowledge about all aspects of computing systems, and their use. In other words, the Computer Scientist is primarily engaged in the discovery of new knowledge about computing, while the Software Engineer is interested in applying that and other knowledge.

There is, in this context, a fundamental difference between the prime objectives of Computer Science and Software Engineering education. In particular Software Engineering education must be concerned with the acquisition of practical skills relating to the use of existing techniques and technologies coupled with the development of managerial skills.

Computer Science education, on the other hand, tends to be biased towards the theoretical issues and the study of existing systems with a view to the development of new concepts and knowledge (See Sommerville pp302-303 [SOM85]).

As an example, one would expect to find the formal study of algorithm and module re-use at a practical level in a Software Engineering course, but one would not be surprised to find such a topic omitted from an undergraduate Computer Science offering.

Further differences are apparent when considering practical assignments offered in each case. Assignments in Computer Science tend to exhibit the following features, as was recently noted by Ciesielski et. al [CIE88]. They tend to be:

a) small individual assignments designed to test ingenuity, or familarise the student with some new technique or language feature,

b) large individual projects,

c) team projects, such as the implementation of a compiler, or a modest commercial system.

Assignments are frequently artificially constructed to meet narrow pedagogic goals, and the results are not used by those other than the developers. However, in DP departments and software houses programmers are required to work as teams, to generate programs and documentation that will be used by others and to define and satisfy the the needs of users, often working from poor specifications. There is frequently a large gap between the educational experience of students and the situation in the work place, as has been noted by other software engineering educators [MCK87], [BUR87], and [FRE87].

In addition, it is not always the case that there are sufficient resources available for detailed verification of a student's submission's correctness. Issues such as modular design, and elementary module reuse are also unlikely to be used as the basis for designing assignments.

The result is that students in a traditional Computer Science degree tend to see a satisfactory program as one which will pass a cursory assessment procedure when tested using selected data.

A Software Engineering programming assignment, on the other hand, may be set to provide experience in some particular technique. In addition, the standard of testing and documentation required may be significantly higher. Ideally, sufficient staff resources should be available to allow incorrect code and poor design to be detected - with students being asked to correct deficiencies for a passing grade.

Software Engineering practical work may also contain a "maintenance experience", that is, the discovery and correction of errors in some large piece of software (see [TOM87]), some modifications involving the addition of functionality to some previously developed piece of software may be required.

3.3. A Philosophical Basis for Software Engineering Education

The authors of this course proposal have extensive experience as both Computer Science and Software Engineering educators. Both are qualified engineers, and believe that their approaches have been influenced by their respective basic educations. The proposed degree, which will be offered beginning in 1990, is based upon a particular philosophical view of both engineering and Software Engineering[1].

In addition, the syllabus designers, had, as a primary goal, the training of graduates capable of producing high quality software. They were substantially influenced by Parnas' papers [PAR72], by work on both State Transition Diagrams ([DAY70] and [WAS85]) and Petri Net techniques as system design and program implementation techniques [STO89], by Basili's approach to metrics and quality evaluation [BAS85], by Beohm's work on estimating [BEO82] and by Belady's general approach to Software Engineering. Other techniques emphasized include modular programming[2] and interpretive and table-driven systems.

The philosophical underpinning of our syllabi can be summarized as follows, although the priority is not necessarily absolute:

- **We assume that product and design re-use are the fundamental means of achieving effective software development (see [SIL85]).** *This leads us to promote modular design, data-driven programming techniques and the acquisition of a wide range of algorithmic techniques.*

- **We assume that Software Engineers require an extensive knowledge of traditional system description techniques.** *This leads us to include the study of a variety of description and development methodologies usually associated with commercial systems analysis.*

- **We assume that quantative measures of product and project quality and behavior are important.** *This leads us to treat software metrics, project structure and organization, software testing* [MYE79], *and reliability.*

- **We assume that tools are essential means of increasing software productivity.** *This leads us to study their design and use.*

- **We assume that effective specification of software is a prerequisite to good design.** *This leads to the study of formal and informal analysis and specification techniques, and to the study of prototyping techniques(see* [CAR83] *).*

- **We assume that effective project management is necessary.** *This leads us to the study of estimating techniques, estimating, project management and the software process.*

---

[1] The first author has nine years experience in conducting a three subject undergraduate major in SE in a prior incarnation, while the second author has extensive experience with the use of protocol engineering and reliability engineering techniques in large scale software development.

[2] The first author was substantially influenced by early experience with the KDF9 K Autocode and IBM Fortran 4-E subroutine libraries in the mid 1960's.

- **We assume that a wide knowledge of programming languages and utilities such as database and operating system interfaces is required.** *This leads us to the study of database and operating systems,*

and finally,

- **We assume that a Software Engineer should have a good general Computer Science education.** *Which means that the course contains a complete undergraduate major on Computer Science[3].*

This material is spread throughout the course in a manner intended to develop both practical and theoretical skills.

4. THE DEGREE STRUCTURE

All students undertake a common first and second year, which includes Software Engineering related material in Computer Science I (about 10%), and in Computer Systems Engineering II (about 50%).

Students specialize in third and fourth year, with all candidates taking Computer Science III and components of Computer Systems Engineering III in third year. Fourth year Software Engineering majors take only Computer Science and Software Engineering. This is shown in a little meore detail in Table I.

As already discussed, all students other than the Software Engineering majors take a Software Engineering team project in third year. The latter under take their project in fourth year as part of Software Engineering IV, and operate in a Software Hut mode.

5. THE SOFTWARE ENGINEERING MAJOR STREAM

5.1. First Year

First year students are introduced to some basic Software Engineering topics. These include an introduction to

a)   the Waterfall model of the software process [AGR86],

b)   modular design, information hiding concepts, and the use of existing modules,

c)   simple prescriptive testing procedures [MYE79],

---

[3] The normal undergraduate major offered by LTU would occupy about 30% of the students total load over three years. As such, it is used as the basis for the BSE degree.

TABLE I. SUBJECTS IN THE BCSE DEGREE

First Year   (4.5 UNITS)   (COMMON)

Electronics I	(1.0)
Physics ICS*	(0.5)
Computer Science I	(1.0)
Computer Systems I	(0.5)
Mathematics IA	(1.0)
Mathematics IDM	(0.5)

Second Year   (3.5 UNITS)   (COMMON)

Electronics II	(1.0)
Applied Maths II	(0.5)
Computer Systems Engineering II*	(1.0)
Computer Science II	(1.0)

MAJOR STREAMS

Third Year   (2.4 Units)

Software Engineering		Digital Computer Engineering		Network Engineering	
Computer Sci. IIIA*	(0.8)	Computer Sci. III	(1.0)	Computer Sci. III	(1.0)
Comp. Sys. Eng. IIIB	(0.5)	Comp. Sys. Eng. IIIB	(0.5)	Comp. Sys. Eng. IIIA*	(0.5)
Software Eng. III*	(0.7)	Comp. Sys. Eng IIIB*	(0.5)	Comp. Sys. Eng. IIIC*	(0.5)
Statistics IIICS*	(0.2)	Statistics IIICS*	(0.2)	Statistics IIICS*	(0.2)
Soc. Imp. of Eng. *	(0.2)	Soc. Imp. of Eng. *	(0.2)	Soc. Imp. of Eng. *	(0.2)

Fourth Year   (1.25 Units)

Software Engineering		Digital Computer Engineering		Network Engineering	
Comp. Sci. IVA*	(0.50)	Comp. Sci. IVA*	(0.50)	Comp. Sci. IVA*	(0.50)
Software Eng. IV	(0.50)	Comp. Sys. Eng. IVA*	(0.25)	Comp. Sys. Eng. IVA*	(0.25)
Comp. Sys. Proj. IV*	(0.25)	Comp. Sys. Eng. IVB*	(0.25)	Comp. Net. Eng. IV*	(0.25)
		Comp. Sys. Proj. IV*	(0.25)	Comp. Sys. Proj. IV*	(0.25)

* New Subjects

d)   informal specification techniques,

and

e)   an analysis-synthesis approach to program design which maximizes simple module re-use.

It should be kept in mind that ALL Computer Science students take Computer Science I, and therefore take some basic Software Engineering.

The subject Computer Systems I contains material on graphics, human interfaces, C and other topics.

5.2. Second Year

Computer Systems Engineering II is, as already mentioned, roughly 50% Software Engineering, allowing 4 hours of lectures per week for two semesters. The course focuses on the following topics, building on earlier material:

a)   System description techniques, such as Data Flow Diagrams, Jackson's methodology [JAC83], structure charts etc.,

b)   Modular programming,

c)   Object Oriented approaches,

d)   Macrogenerators,

e)   Database systems and their interfaces,

f)   Operating System interfaces,

g)   Transportability and practical algorithm reuse.

Students also take Computer Science II which is a fairly conventional second year course.

5.3. Third Year

Students majoring in Software Engineering take Software Engineering III, Computer Science IIIA, Statistics IIICS and Social Implications of Engineering, as well as Computer Systems Engineering IIIB, which is an advanced computer architecture unit.

Software Engineering III deals in depth with a substantial body of the discipline, supporting lectures with practical assignments designed to demonstrate the value of the techniques presented. A total of four hours of lectures are available each week, for two semesters.

Topics presented include:

a) Software metrics, both structure and quality,

b) System description techniques, such as State Transition Diagrams, the NEC SPD and others [AZU85],

c) Interpretive and table-driven programming techniques, and co-routines

d) Productivity issues, software and process re-use, fourth generation and special purpose languages, application generators,

e) Software Security and Reliability,

f) Transportability, "virtual" systems, operating system interfaces,

g) System partitioning issues, eg IBM SAA

h) Test coverage metrics, software maintenance and modifiability

Computer Science III contains a wide range of components which complement the Software Engineering material. Students taking the Software Engineering major must take Computer Science IIIA, which consists of units in Fourth Generation Languages and in Business Management, as well as six other components from the rest of that offering. Available topics include Parallel Computing, Formal languages, Graphics, Artificial Intelligence[4], and Workload Analysis.

Statistics IIICS deals with queuing theory and related material, and is one hour per week for the whole year, while Social Implications of Engineering addresses ethics, environmental and other issues relevant to the relationship between Engineering and society.

5.4. Fourth Year

The final Software Engineering subject serves two purposes, and runs for two semesters at four hours per week. The first is to introduce the student to advanced topics likely to be influencing the future directions of the field, while the second is to provide

---

[4] AI is also introduced in first year.

practical knowledge of estimating and project management techniques.

Again, students must take Computer Science IVA, which is a selection of the standard Honours year offering, including the Advanced Software Engineering component therein.

Software Engineering IV proposes to deal with:

a)   Formal Methods,

b)   CASE tools and their history,

c)   Impact of system structure on functionality and performance,

d)   Software reliability,

e)   Software quality control and measurement, including the TAME concept (see Basili and Rombach [BAS88]),

f)   Computer resource usage, monitoring and estimation,

g)   Contractual and project management issues,

h)   Configuration management and version control,

i)   Information and Data Engineering,

j)   System testing

k)   Application of A.I. to software engineering,

l)   Experimental methods and data collection.

Final year students also complete a major project which will be a team project, run on Software Hut lines.

6. CONCLUSION

The Software Engineering course outlined above will produce graduates able to make a substantial contribution to solving the Software crisis. We see no real difficulty in mounting the Degree, and are confident that students will be able to cope with the subject matter. We also believe we have demonstrated that an undergraduate program in Software Engineering is readily achievable.

In addition, we submit that the ease with which we were able to identify material for our syllabi is ample proof that we have a discipline mature enough to warrant such a course.

7. ACKNOWLEDGEMENTS

The author's would like to acknowledge those members of the Department of Computer Science who assisted in the design and construction of the Degree. Special thanks are due to Dr. Rhys Francis and Dr. Ian Robinson for assisting in ensuring that the proposal met the requirements of the University's various committees. Our thanks also go Ms. Kit Martin, Ms. Colleen Pearce and Ms. M. Clamp who prepared the various documents that were needed. Thanks are also due to our colleagues in the Electronic Engineering Department for their stimulating comments and advice.

In the end, however, the views expressed in this paper are the authors, and any errors or omissions are their responsibility.

REFERENCES

[AGR86]   Agresti, W.W. "The Conventional Software Life-cycle Model: Its Evolution and Assumptions", in IEEE Tutorial on New Paradigms for Software Development, Agretsi, W. W. (ed) 1986 pp. 2-6

[ARD85]   Ardis, M., Brouhana, J., Fairley, R., Gerhardt, S., Martin, N., and McKeeman, W. "Core Course Documentation: Master's Degree Program in Software Engineering". School of Information Technology, Wang Inst. Graduate Studies Tech. Report TR-65-17 Sept. 1985

[ARD87]   Ardis, M. "The Evolution of the Wang Institute's Master of Software Engineering Program", IEEE Trans. on Software Engineering vol. SE-13 no. 11 1987

[AZU85]   Azuma, M., Tabata, T., Oki, Y. and Kamiya, S. "SPD: A Humanized Documentation Technology", IEEE Trans. on Software Engineering vol. SE-11 no. 9 Sep. 1985 pp. 945-953

[BAS85]   Basili, V.R. "Quantitative Evaluation of S.E. Methodology", (Keynote Address) Proc. First Pan Pacific Computer Conference, Melbourne Australia, Sep. 1985

[BAS88]   Basili, V.R. and Rombach, H.D. "The TAME Project: Towards Improvement-Oriented Software Environments", IEEE Trans. on Software Engineering vol. SE-14 no. 6 Jun 1988 pp. 758-773

[BEO82]   Boehm, B.W. "Software Engineering Economics", Prentice-Hall 1982

[BUR87]   Burns, J.E. and Robertson, E.L. "Tow Complementary Course Sequences on the Design and Implementation of Software Products", IEEE Trans. on Software Engineering vol. SE-13 no.11 1987

[CAR83]   Carey, T.T., and Mason, R.E.A. "Information System Prototyping: Techniques, Tools, Methodologies", INFOR - Canadian Journal of Computational Research and Information Processing Vol. 21 No. 3 May 1983 pp. 177-191

[CIE88]   Ciesielski, V.R., Reed, K. and Cybulski, J.L., "Experience with a Project Oriented Course in Software Engineering", Proc. of the Australian Software Engineering Conference (ASWEC), May 1988 pp. 125-131

[DAY70]

Day, A.C. "The use of symbol-state tables", Computer Journal Vol. 13 No. 4, Nov 1970

[FAI85]   Fairley, R.E. "Software Engineering Concepts", McGraw-Hill 1985

[FAI87]   Fairley, R.E. "Guest Editor's Introduction", IEEE Trans. on Software Engineering vol. SE-13 No. 11 Nov. 1987 pp. 1141-1142, Special Issues on Software Engineering Education

[FOR89]   Ford, G.A. and Gibbs, N.E. "A Master of Software Engineering Curriculum", IEEE Computer, vol. 22 no. 9, Sep. 1989 pp. 59-71

[FRE87]   Freeman, P. "Essential Elements of Software Engineering Education Revisited", IEEE Trans. on Software Engineering vol. SE-13 no. 11 Nov 1987 pp.1143-1148

[GIB89a]   Gibbs, N.E. "The SEI Education Program: The Challenge of Teaching Future Software Engineers", Comm ACM, Vol. 32 No. 5, May 1989 pp. 594-605

[GIB89b]   Gibbs, N.E. "Is the Time Right for an Undergraduate Software Engineering Degree?" in Proc. Software Engineering Education Conference July 1989, Springer-Verlag LCNS 376, Gibbs, N. E. (ed)

[HAW88]   Hawryszkiewycz, I.T. "Introduction to Systems Analysis and Design", Prentice-Hall 1988

[HOR77]   Horning, J.J. and Wortman, D.B. "Software Hut: A computer program engineering project in the form of a game", IEEE Trans. on Software Engineering vol. SE-3 No. 4 Jul 1977 pp325-330

[JAC83]   Jackson, M.A. "System Development", Prentice-Hall 1983

[LEE81]   Lee, K.Y. "Status of Graduate Software Engineering Education", Proc. ACM81

[MCK87]   McKeeman, W.M. "Experience with a software engineering project course", IEEE Trans. on Software Engineering vol. SE-13 no. 11 Nov 1987 pp. 1182-1192

[MYE79]   Myers, G.J. "The Art of Software Testing", Wiley, 1979

[PAR72]   Parnas, D.L. "On the criteria to used in decomposing systems into modules", Comm ACM, vol. 15 no. 2 1972

[PRE88]   Pressman, R.S. "Software Engineering, A Practitioners Approach", McGraw-Hill,1988

[REE87]   Reed, K. "Commercial Software Engineering, the Way Forward",
           Keynote Address to the Australian Software Engineering Conference
           (ASWEC) Cnaberra, May 1987

[SIL85]   Siverman, B.C. "Software Cost and Productivity Improvements: An
           Analogical View" IEEE Computer Vol. 18 No. 5 May 1985 pp. 86-96

[SOM85]   Sommerville, I. "Software Engineering", 2nd ed. Addison-Wesley,
           1985

[TOM87]   Tomayko, J.E. "Teaching Maintenance Using Large Software
           Artifacts", Proc. Software Education Conference Pittsburgh July
           1989 Springer Verlag LNCS 376 pp. 3-15

[WAS85]   Wasserman, A.I. "Extended State Transitions diagrams for the
           Specification of Human Computer interfaces", IEEE Trans. on
           Software Engineering vol. SE-11 no. 8 1985

Introduction of Software Engineering Concepts in an Ada-Based Introductory Computer Science Course

Frances L. Van Scoy
West Virginia University

Abstract. *An Ada-based introductory computer science course is described. This course attempts to introduce some basic software engineering concepts such as abstraction, information hiding, object-oriented development, and software reuse.*

1. Background

West Virginia University is a comprehensive, land-grant university of approximately 17,000 students. The Department of Statistics and Computer Science offers degrees in computer science at the bachelors, masters, and doctoral levels. There are generally about 80 students enrolled in the introductory course for majors during fall semester.

When the department was established in the late 1960's, the language taught in the introductory course was FORTRAN. In approximately 1973 PL/I was chosen as the language taught in the first course and emphasized throughout the undergraduate program. In recent years other languages were used in junior and senior level courses, but freshmen and sophomores used PL/I primarily.

Faculty in the department, however, have been interested in Ada for nearly a decade. In summer 1980 a unit on Ada tasking was taught in a graduate course in parallel processing. Then in spring 1981 two faculty members taught a noncredit continuing education Ada course which was attended by many students, faculty, and staff. Units on Ada in both required and elective courses have been taught repeatedly since then. A junior-level elective in Ada and object-oriented development was first offered in 1986.

At the request of the Software Engineering Institute, during spring semester 1987 the department taught our introductory computer science course in Ada using Heath computing systems and Alsys Ada compilers supplied by the SEI. The course did not run as smoothly as our usual introductory course. (For example, no text book was ordered due to the short lead time, and few undergraduate students with sufficient Ada skills were available to serve as student consultants.) However, the experiment did demonstrate that Ada could be taught to freshmen and did encourage us to begin planning for eventually adopting Ada as the primary language taught by the department.

During spring 1989 the department voted to adopt Ada as the primary programming language in the undergraduate curriculum. Beginning with fall semester 1989 the required sequence of courses for freshman majors is taught using Ada.

This paper describes our design for an Ada-based introductory course which was taught for the first time during fall semester, 1989.

2. Philosophy of the Course

We believe students should be taught a proper software engineering mindset from the beginning of their computing education. For this reason, the course emphasizes abstraction, information hiding, object-oriented development, and software reuse.

Typically half of our entering majors have no computing experience. Additionally, we believe that students need some concrete experiences in a discipline before studying abstract principles. Because of this, the first course emphasizes Ada software development.

The course begins with concepts which are rarely found outside of Ada and Modula-2 in the expectation that students with previous computing experience might find their old ways of developing software inadequate and be encouraged to learn the new ways presented in the course.

Our first course emphasizes reading Ada code before writing Ada code in the belief that an individual learns a natural language by first hearing or reading many spoken or written examples in that language and then learns grammar and vocabulary formally.

The increasing emphasis in industry on reusability has led to the decision that our students will begin their software development education by modifying existing Ada code.

Because Ada software must be developed according to some design method, many of the examples with which the students work have been developed by using a method such as OOD or PAMELA.

Our students will be expected to write complete programs in later courses and on part-time jobs beginning with the sophomore year. To help prepare our students for this work, the course also teaches them how to write complete Ada programs.

3. Design of Course

The course is strongly example-based.

We believe that students deal with programming language features at several levels:
(1) observing language features,
(2) using (and understanding) software written by others and using particular language features,
(3) designing software which uses these features, and
(4) implementing software which uses these features.
As a result the course presents various language features at several of these levels.

Administrative Details of Course. The course is taught in two 75-minute lecture periods and one 100-minute recitation/laboratory period each week for fifteen weeks.

The textbook adopted is *Ada from the Beginning*, written by Jan Skansholm and published by Addison Wesley in 1988.

Students use a Vax cluster, the VMS operating system, the Digital Ada Compilation System, and the EDT text editor.

Organization of Course. The course as originally planned is organized into six units, with a full lecture period test after each of the first five units and a comprehensive final examination at the end of the course.

Each lecture is strongly based on a collection of sample Ada subprograms and packages. The students are given printed copies of the examples and have access to machine readable versions. The following outline shows the titles of the 25 course lectures and their grouping into units.

Unit 1 -- Using Packages

1. Using Packages and Procedures
2. Using Parameters
3. Using Declarations of Objects
4. Using Loops (loop...exit when...end loop;)
5. Using Generic Packages

Unit 2 -- Writing Subprograms

6. Expressions and Assignments
7. TEXT_IO
8. Conditionals
9. Loops
10. Writing Subprograms

Unit 3 -- Designing Packages

11. Designing Packages

12. Writing Package Specifications
13. Private and Limited Private Types

Unit 4 -- Designing and Implementing using Types

14. Scalar Types and Their Attributes
15. Record Types and Their Attributes
16. Access Types and Their Attributes
17. Array Types and Their Attributes
18. Subtypes and Derived Types

Unit 5 -- Implementing Packages

19. Using Exceptions
20. Writing Package Bodies
21. Writing Generic Units
22. Order of Compilation

Unit 6 -- Using Concurrency

23. Observing Tasks
24. Using Tasks
25. Writing Tasks

The next few sections of this paper describe specific details of portions of these units.

Unit 1 -- Using Packages. A major goal of the first unit is to accustom the students to using Ada packages written by others.

Problems including ordering food at a restaurant, printing banners, writing form letters, using a calculator, and drawing simple pictures (based on straight lines and circles, for printing on a conventional line printer) were presented. During the five class meetings of the unit several packages for each problem were presented to illustrate calls of parameterless procedures, calls of procedures with parameters, declaration of objects, use of simple loops (without iteration control, with exit statement), and instantiation of generic packages. During this unit students were given listings of specifications and bodies of all packages but only the specifications were discussed in class.

In the fifth lecture, students were shown the following specification of a generic package. The private part of the package specification was not discussed.)

```
generic
        type ELEMENT is private;
        with procedure GET(VALUE: out ELEMENT );
        with procedure PUT(VALUE: in ELEMENT );
        with function "<"(X:  in ELEMENT; Y: in ELEMENT)
                return BOOLEAN;
```

```
package COLLECTION_2 is
        type OBJECT is private;
        procedure PUT_FIRST_VALUE(
                OF_COLLECTION: in out OBJECT);
        procedure PUT_NEXT_VALUE(
                OF_COLLECTION: in out OBJECT);
        function THERE_IS_ANOTHER_VALUE(
                OF_COLLECTION: in OBJECT)
                        return BOOLEAN;
        procedure THIS_IS_FIRST(VALUE: in ELEMENT ;
                OF_THIS_COLLECTION: in out OBJECT);
        procedure THIS_IS_NEXT(VALUE: in ELEMENT ;
                OF_THIS_COLLECTION: in out OBJECT);
        procedure SET_TO_EMPTY(
                THIS_COLLECTION: in out OBJECT);
        procedure COPY_CONTENTS(
                OF_THIS_COLLECTION: in OBJECT;
                TO_THIS_COLLECTION: out OBJECT);
        function IS_EMPTY(THIS_COLLECTION: in OBJECT)
                        return BOOLEAN;
        procedure FIND_AND_REMOVE_SMALLEST_VALUE(
                OF_THIS_COLLECTION: in out OBJECT;
                WHICH_IS: out ELEMENT );
        NO_MORE_ELEMENTS : exception;
private
        type VALUE_ARRAY is array (1..100) of ELEMENT ;
        type OBJECT is
                record
                        THE_VALUE: VALUE_ARRAY;
                        LENGTH: INTEGER := 0;
                        POSITION_OF_CURRENT_ELEMENT: INTEGER
                                := 0;
                end record;
end COLLECTION_2;
```

In this example students were introduced informally to operations which are constructors, selectors, or iterators. Also, they were shown how to write a procedure which uses an expansion of this package to sort a collection of integers. Because of the abstraction used, students were able to write a sorting program without knowing about arrays or linked lists. (At this stage in the course the students were presented some information about how to instantiate a generic unit but not how to build the specification or body of one.)

In laboratory and on quizzes and the unit test, students were expected to be able to respond to an assignment by choosing an appropriate package or packages from those provided by the instructor and writing a procedure which used that package (or packages) to accomplish the required job. This suggests that students were expected to develop in the first few weeks of the course a sense of when a driver procedure needs the ability to remember results of procedure calls and when iteration is appropriate. Also, one question on the first test this semester asked the student to use an instructor-provided package which implemented the abstract data type STRING (varying length) with an instantiation of package COLLECTION_2 in implementing a sort of a collection of strings.

Unit 2 -- Writing Subprograms. This unit was presented in a fairly traditional fashion.

Unit 3 -- Designing Packages. Students were shown many examples of four uses of packages (Booch, 1987a):

(1) named collections of declarations
(2) groups of related program units
(3) abstract data types
(4) abstract state machines.

Students were shown the following specification as one example of a package implementation of an abstract state machine.

```
package GASOLINE_TANK is
        procedure FILL_IT_UP;
                -- fills car's gasoline tank with gasoline
        procedure DRIVE(MILES: in FLOAT);
                -- simulates driving car distance MILES
        procedure READ_OWNERS_MANUAL(
                SIZE_OF_TANK_IN_GALLONS: out FLOAT);
                -- indicates capacity of gasoline tank in gallons
        function CONTENTS return FLOAT;
                -- returns amount of gasoline in tank as a percentage
        YOU_RAN_OUT_OF_GAS: exception;
                -- raised when gasoline tank becomes empty
end GASOLINE_TANK;
```

They were then given this assignment:

Write an Ada procedure which uses this package and does the following:
(1) does whatever you think appropriate (by use of resources in package GASOLINE_TANK) to gather needed information,
(2) inputs the number of miles to be traveled, and
(3) simulates driving that many miles and filling the gasoline tank of the car as needed to assure that the car never runs out of gas.

Lectures also presented definitions of kinds of objects (actor, agent, server) and kinds of operations (constructor, selector, iterator) (Booch, 1987b). Previous examples were discussed in terms of these kinds of objects and operations. An informal presentation of object-oriented development based on the paragraph approach was also given.

Unit 4 -- Designing and Implementing using Types. The emphases in this unit are on the attributes and operations provided for each kind of type and on how to decide which kind of type is the appropriate one to use.

Many of the examples presented in lecture were packages which implemented various abstract data types. Two of these examples were postal addresses (implemented by record types) and model trains (implemented by record and access types).

On the unit test, students were asked to modify a package implementing a calendar date by adding functions which extract a month name, day, or year from a date. They were also asked to use resources provided by several packages presented in lecture to represent the information needed for a driver's license and to print a license.

Unit 5 -- Implementing Packages. This unit deals with rather specific details of the Ada language such as exception handlers, parameters for generic units, and the order of compilation of Ada units.

As in the previous unit, the emphasis of the lectures on generic units was on the selection of the appropriate data types. Some examples illustrated the use of attributes of discrete types and the need for explicit type conversion when multiplying two values of a fixed point type. These examples helped to reinforce concepts presented in the previous unit.

Lecture material on exception handling was derived from a tutorial by Brosgol (1986). Only the simpler concepts were presented.

Unit 6 -- Using Concurrency. This short unit was planned (1) to introduce the remaining Ada unit, the task, not presented previously and (2) to support future course development. Some faculty teaching this course believe that freshmen enter the first course with an essentially concurrent view of the physical world. If so, this concurrent view should be encouraged by early use of the features of Ada which support concurrent algorithms. Future versions of this introductory course may introduce concurrency at an early point in the semester.

As planned, this final unit of the course will merely show students some examples of interesting use of Ada tasks and will not expect the students to be able to design and implement tasks on their own.

Students will be shown examples of tasks which implement concurrent algorithms. They will also be shown examples of tasks which are used to control the order in which operations are carried out. The following excerpt from an example shows that a bank account must be opened before any other operations on the account are allowed. Any number of deposits, withdrawals, and balance inquiries are then allowed before the account is closed.

```
task body BANK is
begin
```

```
select
     accept OPEN_ACCOUNT(INITIAL_DEPOSIT: in MONEY) do
          BALANCE := INITIAL_DEPOSIT;
     end OPEN_ACCOUNT;
or
     accept DEPOSIT(AMOUNT: in MONEY) do
          PUT_MESSAGE_ACCOUNT_HAS_NOT_BEEN_OPENED;
     end DEPOSIT;
or
     accept WITHDRAW(AMOUNT: in MONEY) do
          PUT_MESSAGE_ACCOUNT_HAS_NOT_BEEN_OPENED;
     end WITHDRAW;
or
     accept REQUEST_BALANCE(AMOUNT: out MONEY) do
          AMOUNT := ZERO;
          PUT_MESSAGE_ACCOUNT_HAS_NOT_BEEN_OPENED;
     end REQUEST_BALANCE;
or
     accept CLOSE_ACCOUNT(AMOUNT: out MONEY) do
          AMOUNT := ZERO;
          PUT_MESSAGE_ACCOUNT_HAS_NOT_BEEN_OPENED;
     end CLOSE_ACCOUNT;
end select;
loop
     select
          accept OPEN_ACCOUNT(
                    INITIAL_DEPOSIT: in MONEY) do
                    PUT_MESSAGE_ACCOUNT_ALREADY_EXISTS;
          end OPEN_ACCOUNT;
     or
          accept DEPOSIT(AMOUNT: in MONEY) do
               BALANCE := BALANCE + AMOUNT;
          end DEPOSIT;
     or
          when BALANCE > ZERO =>
             accept WITHDRAW(
                              AMOUNT: in MONEY) do
                    if BALANCE >= AMOUNT then
                         BALANCE :=

                                          BALANCE - AMOUNT;
                    else
                         PUT_MESSAGE_INSUFFICIENT_BALANCE;
                    end if;
               end WITHDRAW;
     or
          accept REQUEST_BALANCE(
                    AMOUNT: out MONEY) do
               PUT_MESSAGE_BALANCE_IS(AMOUNT);
          end REQUEST_BALANCE;
```

```
or
            accept CLOSE_ACCOUNT(AMOUNT: out MONEY) do
                       PUT_MESSAGE_CLOSING_ACCOUNT(AMOUNT);
            end CLOSE_ACCOUNT;
            exit;
        end select;
    end loop;
  end BANK;
```

This unit was not taught, however, during fall 1989 primarily because of lack of faculty time to prepare strong examples. We anticipate that the unit will be available for use when the course is taught in spring 1990.

4. Observations

The tone of the course varies deliberately from unit to unit from practical examples based on abstract ideas; to straightforward use of statements common to most languages; to abstract discussion of objects, operations, abstract data types, and abstract state machines; to decision making based on theoretical concepts (in choice of kind of type); to practical issues of using Ada (such as order of compilation and rules for parameters of generic units); to examples of the use of Ada tasks.

During the first unit, students with no background in programming seemed more comfortable than those with previous programming experience. The experienced students at times expressed concern about not knowing how to write stand-alone programs. The anxiety level of the experienced students seemed to be reduced somewhat by the provision of the text of the bodies of all packages discussed in class even though those bodies contained language features not yet presented in class.

In the second unit, experienced students relaxed noticeably as they recognized familiar concepts and gained the ability to write complete programs. The discomfort of the first three weeks did seem to result in the students realizing from the beginning, however, that Ada is a different language from those they have previously studied and requires a different approach for software design.

Since students learned key vocabulary and concepts in unit three, unit four was taught at a fairly high level with an emphasis on the kinds of operations and attributes available for each kind of type and the implications for the implementor in defining a type.

Presentation of the material for unit five required more time than originally anticipated.

5. Early Thoughts of Evaluation

Since the course has being taught in this form for only one semester, it is hard to make specific statements about the degree of success of the course. However, some general comments can be made.

Because the students are able to use instructor-provided packages which implement data structures at a higher level than arrays, they are gaining skills in implementing algorithms at a fairly high level of abstraction. However this gain is at the expense of the strong experience in using arrays which is typical of a traditional introductory course.

The course emphasizes abstraction, information hiding, object-oriented development, and software reuse. If the course is successful, students will leave the course with the expectation that their future software development will involve the use of well-defined software development methods, the building of abstractions, and the reuse of software. We expect that in upper division courses in which a project is required students will be able to build more sophisticated projects with less overall effort by the reuse of generic units, for example. (All of our undergraduates build a compiler, a data base management system, and an operating system as juniors or seniors.)

Most importantly, students are being taught in a natural fashion from the beginning of their computing education to reason about software. They are being taught to think in terms of abstract data types and abstract state machines and to reason about operations appropriate to a particular user-defined type. We look forward to building on this foundation in subsequent courses.

Bibliography

Booch, Grady (1987a). *Software Engineering with Ada, second edition.* Benjamin/Cummings.

Booch, Grady (1987b). *Software Components with Ada: Structures, Tools, and Subsystems.* Benjamin/Cummings.

Brosgol, Benjamin M. (1986) *Tutorial on Exception Handling in Ada.* Proceedings of the Washington Ada Symposium, Washington, D.C..

Skansholm, Jan (1988). Ada from the Beginning. Addison Wesley.

Teaching Reuse Early

Viswa Santhanam
Boeing Military Airplanes

Abstract: *Computer science graduates are ill-prepared to take on the software engineering challenges facing the industry. To bridge this gap, it is necessary to change the way the students are trained to approach the software engineering problem. Reuse should be addressed from the outset as a principal programming technique in order to avoid a detrimental mindset. This paper presents a model first programming course based on Ada which seeks to promote the practice of reuse through carefully chosen programming assignments.*

1.   Introduction

The gap between computer science education and software engineering practice has been noted elsewhere [1]. One of the contributing factors is that the typical CS graduate has not practiced the kind of software engineering methodology that the industry practices or, more accurately, strives to practice. In spite of many attempts to introduce a flavor of industrial practice into academic training [1,2], the gap remains. In particular, techniques for programming-in-the-large, such as reuse and rapid prototyping, are virtually unknown to the new hires. This paper addresses the need for teaching reuse early on in the undergraduate curriculum in an effort to bridge the gap.

2.   Importance of Early Reuse Education

Effective practice of software reuse faces many technical, psychological, political and organizational obstacles [3]. Most of the research in reuse has been aimed at solving the technical challenges. Political and organizational barriers are beyond the scope of this work. There are, however, some psychological hurdles which deserve attention but have largely been ignored by the software research community. One of those hurdles is the "mindset" that forms early in the programming career, ominous signs of which can be seen in the inability of seasoned programmers to make effective judgements about reuse [4] and in the so-called "Not-Invented-Here" syndrome [5].

Virtually all computer science undergraduate programs in the U.S. begin with programming in some high-level language and most of them never make the transition into programming-in-the-large. The MSE program recommended by the SEI includes two courses--*Software generation* and *Software design*-- which deal with reuse [1]. But addressing reuse at the graduate level is too late for a couple of reasons:

(1)   Not all programmers involved in large software projects will go to graduate school;

(2)   Having practiced coding at the lines-of-code level for several years, learning to program at the modules level requires breaking a deep-rooted habit of preferring new code to existing code.

The *status quo* is not entirely inexplicable. There have been genuine difficulties in introducing hands-on reuse in the classroom:

(1)   Availability of suitable programming languages to support reuse;

(2)   The short duration (one quarter or semester) of most programming courses which encourages the use of shorter assignments;

(3)   Lack of incentive to reuse (e.g., short and unrelated assignments make it difficult and/or unnecessary to reuse earlier products);

(4)   Lack of libraries of reusable modules (few schools have made commercial libraries available to students);

(5)   Lack of tools to practice programming at the module level (module composition tools often depend on expensive workstations);

(6)   Instructor's own mindset;

(7)   High turn over among the faculty which results in loss of continuity in course contents and, therefore, diminishes the opportunity to build a rich library of reusable modules for students to access.

Many of these obstacles are diminishing with emerging technology and improving economic basis for computer science programs. For example, schools that have made the transition from Pascal or Fortran to Ada as the programming language of choice have fewer concerns with issues 1 and 4. Some schools, such as Arizona State University, have already addressed issue 2 and introduced programming projects that span multiple semesters. Rapidly dropping workstation prices should help offset concern 5, while general maturing of the technology and better planning on the part of the instructor should help overcome obstacles 2, 3 and 6. The difficulty with faculty turn over will be partly offset by the emergence of "standard" course modules and curriculum recommendations such as the SEI's MSE.

If all of the above obstacles are overcome today, are we prepared to introduce reuse in our undergraduate CS curriculum? The purpose of this article is to outline a model course based on Ada to make that possible. The outline is based on the material developed at the SEI for a second programming course using Ada [6].

3. A Model Ada Course

This section outlines an undergraduate programming course based on Ada. The course is conceived to be an early (preferably the first) programming course in the CS curriculum. It follows a syllabus of Ada topics commonly adapted in semester-long Ada programming courses (see table below). The primary difference is in the hands-

Week #	Topic(s)	Assignments
1	History and basic concepts	
2	Lexical elements and syntax	
3	Basic data types and flow control	Program 1
4	Subprograms	
5	Composite types	Program 2
6	Packages	
7	Review/Test	Program 3
8	Data abstraction	Program 4
9	Exception handling	
10	Advanced data types	Program 5
11	Generics	Program 6
12	Tasking	
13	Predefined packages	Program 7
14	Programming-in-the-large	
15	Review/test	Program 8

on programming assignments. The recommended sequence of assignments for this course represents a gradual building up of the level of reuse needed to achieve the goals, as illustrated in figure 1.

The general intent of programming assignments is to reinforce programming concepts through actual implementation experience. The prevalent practice is to use simple, independent assignments designed to concentrate on specific language constructs, such as subprograms, packages, tasks, generics, and so on. This approach has the advantage that the problems can be contrived to illustrate the best use of the respective

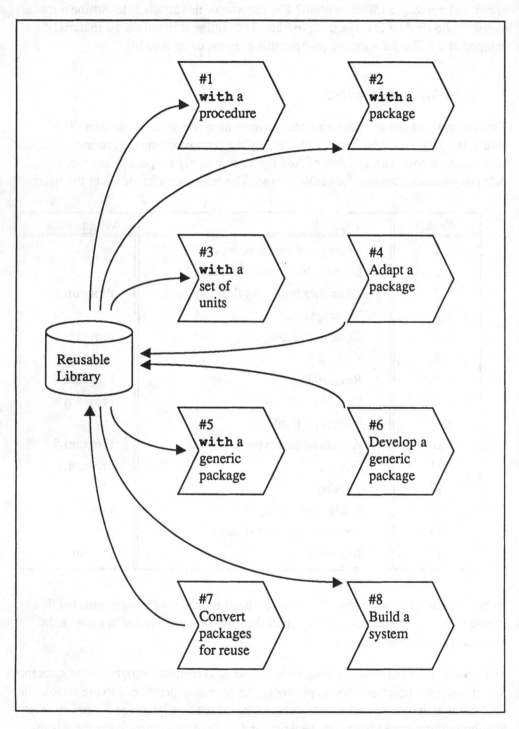

Figure 1. Progressive Reuse in Programming Assignments

constructs in a relatively uncluttered setting. By the same token, the approach has the weakness that it presents a "text book" environment for programming tasks. Besides, the use of language constructs in idealized settings rarely warrants hands-on experience for reinforcement. In any case, such reinforcement should not occur at the expense of experience which will be valuable in real-world programming tasks. Furthermore, the prevalent approach tends to present a close-up view of individual language features, but the more dramatic gains which result from the interplay of several language features tend to be ignored. The proposed sequence of assignments attempts to overcome these pitfalls.

Ada's approach to i/o necessitates even the first programming assignment to rely on predefined packages to display its results. But, most often, the beginning programmer ends up **with**ing TEXT_IO without knowledge of the profound amount of code accounted for in that package. To make the case for reuse more directly, the proposed assignment sequence begins with a problem that would require the use of an independently developed subprogram, such as a sort procedure.

The second assignment takes a step forward by **with**ing a package consisting of several subprograms and data objects. A good package to use might be a data abstraction package for stacks or queues, which is particularly suited if a commercial library is available for class use. The package specification should be discussed in class to drive home the point about the separation of interface and implementation which is essential to software reuse.

The third assignment is an extension of the second to reinforce the notion that in real-world reuse several independent packages may be brought to bear on a single application. The application itself need not be too complex; one that uses both the library subprogram of assignment 1 and the package of assignment 2 should be sufficient.

The fourth assignment aims to paint a realistic picture of reuse as a programming technique in the real world. Unfortunately, it is often necessary to modify existing "reusable" modules before they can be reused. A simple way to achieve this is to require the use of the library subprogram of assignment 1 for a different data type. This choice will also set the stage for introducing Ada generics in the next assignment.

Assignment 5 introduces the notion of generics in Ada. At this time, the unit to be used need not be very complex. The idea to be conveyed is that there is a powerful way to write adaptable modules in Ada, which could be achieved by introducing a generic version of the library unit employed in assignment 1.

Having introduced the flavor of adaptability, the idea of writing generic bodies is addressed next. Converting the package used in assignment 2 or the one adapted by editing in assignment 4 into a generic package would be an appropriate problem for the sixth assignment.

The seventh assignment is intended to address attributes of software fit for reuse. Modules developed up to this point are to be "cleaned up" for reuse, emphasizing documentation, robustness, adaptability and testing.

The final assignment represents an effort to bring together various reuse techniques to build a sizable software system. If the collection of units developed in the preceding assignments is well conceived, this step should clearly show the payoff from reuse.

4.   An Instance of the Model

In this section, a set of specific programing assignments is presented to match the requirements outlined above. The assignments lead to the construction of a library of reusable modules that can be applied to other programming tasks beyond the present course. The goal is to build a reusable Ada package to implement a windowing system for ASCII terminals at the end of the course. The package is to contain primitives needed to create, destroy, open, close (iconize), read from, write to, move, hide and expose an unlimited number of overlapping text windows. The process of building this WINDOWS package is itself based on software reuse notions, as represented in the model course outline.

The first assignment consists of writing a program to draw a rectangle at a specified location using a procedure called GOTOXY which implements random cursor addressing. The GOTOXY procedure is provided by the instructor as a library unit.

The second assignment builds on a package called SCREEN_IO which includes several screen manipulation primitives including random cursor addressing, setting text attributes, saving rectangular areas of text, and so on. Using this package, the student builds the procedures needed to open and close rectangular windows.

The third assignment requires an additional package to manipulate linked lists of windows. A data abstraction package called LISTS is employed to manage a set of overlapping windows. Procedures to create, destroy, hide and expose windows are built in this assignment.

Assignment 4 is a simple variation on the third assignment wherein a substitute for the instructor-supplied LISTS package is obtained by adapting an existing list manipulation package written for integer list elements. Procedures to read from and write to windows are also written.

The fifth assignment replaces the customized LISTS package with a generic package supplied by the instructor. The sixth assignment requires the student to write the implementation for the generic package.

Assignment 7 is aimed at realizing the importance of planning for reuse. The requirements for a reusable WINDOWS package are established. Included in these requirements are data abstraction, proper exception handling, strict documentation and coding standards and testing requirements. The result is a cleaning up of the code (and documentation) developed up to this point so as to meet higher quality metrics.

In the final assignment, the windowing system is demonstrated with an application involving tasking. The dining philosophers problem serves as the backdrop for the auditioning of the windows (see figure 2). Each philosopher task is assigned a window with its banner identifying the owner philosopher. A philosopher who has grabbed both his forks and gets ready to eat will bring his window to the foreground (expose); likewise, when it is time to relinquish the fork and enter the thinking state, he pushes his window to the background (hide). Thus, during the simulation, windows move from foreground to background continually, providing an animation of the tasking program at work.

The final philosopher program, which has the module structure shown in figure 3, has been developed by the author. However, the assignments leading to its construction remain to be tested in the classroom.

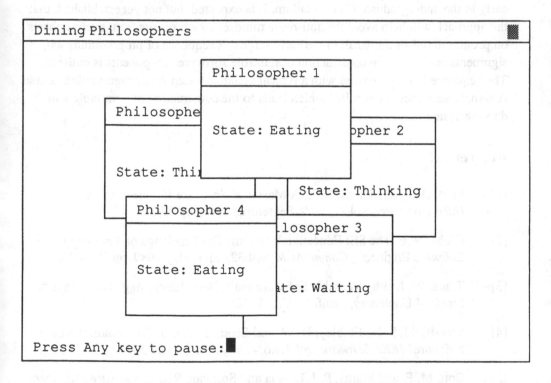

Figure 2. Demonstration of Reusable WINDOWS Package

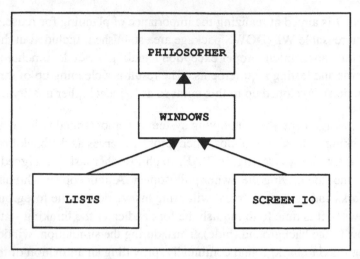

Figure 3. Module structure of Philosopher program

5. Conclusion

A model course based on Ada has been outlined to promote reuse education starting early in the undergraduate CS curriculum. It is expected, but not yet established, that the approach will help avoid the anti-reuse mindset which results from overemphasis on programming-in-the-small in the early stages. A sequence of programming assignments leading to the construction of reusable software components is outlined. The sequence is synchronized with a typical syllabus for an Ada programming course. A sample sequence is described which leads to the construction of a reusable windowing system.

References

[1]   Ford, G. A. and Gibbs, N. E. A Master of Software Engineering Curriculum, *IEEE Computer*, vol.22, no.9, September 1989, pp.59-71.

[2]   Gibbs, N. E. The SEI Education Program: The Challenge of Teaching Future Software Engineers, *Comm. ACM,* vol.32, no.5, May 1989, pp.594-605.

[3]   Tracz, W. J. Why Reusable Software Isn't, Dept. Elec. Engg. Tech. Report, Stanford University, Stanford, CA, 1986.

[4]   Woodfield, S. N., Embley, D. W. and Scott, D. T. Can Programmers Reuse Software? *IEEE Software*, vol.4, no.4, July 1987, pp.52-59.

[5]   Bott, M. F. and Wallis, P. J. L. Ada and Software Reuse, *Software Engineering J.*, September 1988, pp. 177-183.

[6]   Santhanam, V. Introduction to Ada as a Second Language, Course material developed at the SEI, Carnegie-Mellon U., Pittsburg, PA, June 1987.

A State-of-the-Art CS Undergraduate Lab

J. Mack Adams
Barry L. Kurtz
New Mexico State University

Abstract.   *This paper describes the development of a high-quality laboratory for computer science majors over the last decade and plans for its continued development. We start with the historical background and then describe the current situation that involves moving the introductory programming course to Unix workstations. This decision has resulted in many benefits and a few unanticipated problems. Finally, we speculate about future development and describe two possible scenarios: one evolutionary, based on continued adaptation of the original lab concept, and the other revolutionary, based on rethinking the underlying goals of the introductory CS curriculum.*

1. Historical Background

After examining the original goals of the undergraduate lab and how these goals have evolved, we describe the hardware environment and structural organization of the lab. We conclude the section with a description of the computer based software developed to support the introductory programming course.

Goals of the Lab

At its inception in 1978, the laboratory was developed to support the first course for computer science majors, an introduction to problem solving and computer programming using a block-structured language [Adams 81]. One of the major objectives of the lab was to provide sufficient instruction and assistance on programming issues to permit:

- spending more time on conceptual issues in lectures,
- making a rather large final programming assignment feasible, and
- introducing software engineering issues and techniques in the course.

As it turned out, the lab had another very desirable function: providing valuable software engineering experience for upper division undergraduates. This resulted from the way the lab was organized and staffed, as discussed in the next section.

The original lab was used strictly for our introductory programming course. Since that time the lab has expanded to include all of the programming courses in the

undergraduate curriculum, shown in Table 1 in Section 2. This has resulted in some additional objectives:
- access to "bare" machines so that students can learn low level, interrupt-driven programming techniques,
- introduction of alternative programming paradigms (functional, object- oriented, logical) on powerful workstations,
- use of hypertext-like environments using high resolution graphics consoles,
- development of operating systems concepts on Unix PCs,
- use of document preparation software for laser printers, and
- introduction to parallel processing using Ada tasking on a multiprocessor Sequent computer.

These objectives have only been attained with respect to hardware, system software and classroom instruction. As of now, we have no CAI software to support any of these additional objectives. Some of the objectives, such as hypertext-like environments and document preparation software, have been attained simply by making the software available and letting the word spread amongst the students. They train themselves and share "secrets of the trade." In fact, they are becoming so accustomed to large, high resolution displays and laser printers that they often demand more infrastructure support than we can provide.

Hardware and Organizational Structure

The laboratory was conceived on the model of student newspapers -- i.e. it was to be operated and managed by undergraduates for the purpose of serving other undergraduates, but having the side effect of providing the operational/management staff with experience simulating an actual work environment. The enabling technology for this idea was the microcomputer, with relatively tractable software systems and maintenance issues. With the assistance of an Instructional Scientific Equipment Program (ISEP) grant from the NSF, the lab was begun in 1978 and equipped with Terak microcomputers.

For the first two years the lab was operated in a fashion that has now become rather traditional for microcomputer labs, except that all management, operation and maintenance was done by undergraduates under the general supervision of one faculty member. During this period, CAI material was obtained from the University of California at San Diego [Bowles 78] and installed by the staff, as discussed in more detail in the next section.

In the next stage of development, the staff undertook development of our own CAI material and a conversion to the next generation of microcomputers, the IBM PC. This was done with the aid of a Comprehensive Assistance for Undergraduate Education (CAUSE) grant from the NSF. In this stage, the undergraduate staff took considerably more responsibility for providing tutorial assistance, conducting lab tests, and maintaining a larger group of machines. Concomitantly, the responsibilities of the undergraduate managers increased. Perhaps the greatest problem during this stage was the coordination of laboratory and lecture. The initial success of the lab had caused course instructors to neglect coordination somewhat, and with the increased role of the laboratory, it was necessary to establish regular meetings of instructors and teaching assistants with the undergraduate lab director.

For the assembly language and operating systems courses, we obtained support from hardware vendors. The Teraks, originally used for machine organization/assembly language instruction, were replaced by a mixture of Pro 325's and Pro 350's donated by Digital Equipment Corporation. We deliberately chose to remain with a somewhat older architecture for pedagogical reasons. The simplicity of the PDP architecture allows the student to master the architecture and thus builds a level of confidence that we feel would not be achieved with newer architectures.

We received a donation of more than twenty ATT 7300 machines, Unix PCs with hard disks, for use in our operating systems course. Since the types of machines and the number of machines have increased dramatically from the original lab, we no longer use undergraduates for equipment maintenance and system software management. We have established a professionally-staffed computer operations group that, with the aid of hourly undergraduate student employees, provides these functions. However, the management of the lab, the staffing by proctors, and the development of CAI software still remain undergraduate student responsibilities.

Software Development

The programming language initially used in the lab was UCSD Pascal, and CAI software was obtained in 1978 from UCSD to facilitate lab instruction. This included automated objective quizzes and computer tested programming quizzes. The success with these quizzes motivated us to continue development of the material, using development tools obtained from the University of California at Irvine in 1979 [Volper, in print]. In addition to extending and adding to the quizzes, we developed tutorials utilizing the graphics capability of the Teraks and the Irvine development tools. The tutorials were designed by faculty members and implemented by undergraduates in the development group of the laboratory staff [Adams 83]. Some of the CAI material was used for a general education CS course with a laboratory run by the university computer center, as well as the first course for CS majors, and so the material had to meet a fairly high standard of quality and documentation. Portability was also a major concern, as we anticipated that hardware upgrades would occur.

The first hardware upgrade from Teraks to IBM PCs, with second party graphics monitors, severely tested the portability of the software we had developed. Predictably, the part of the conversion dealing with graphics was the most demanding. We had anticipated this by using separate development tools for text and graphics, based on the original tools obtained from Irvine. Although this encapsulated the graphics aspect of the development, apparently minor differences in the bit mapped displays of the Teraks and the IBM PCs and subtle interactions between the text and graphics in the tutorials caused substantial conversion problems. We had estimated the conversion could be done over the summer -- in fact, the conversion lasted well into the fall semester and provided a valuable albeit painful lesson in software engineering for our undergraduate staff.

The next conversion resulted from a software rather than a hardware change. Because of our emphasis on software engineering in the introductory course, we felt the need to change from Pascal to a language with explicit support for modular programming. After weighing the relative merits of the two obvious candidates, Modula-2 and Ada, we decided on Modula-2, although we must admit that our decision was influenced by portability considerations and the absence of a reliable Ada compiler at that time as well as language and pedagogical issues. This conversion was much simpler than the first, primarily because the graphics display aspects did not change. This conversion provided our undergraduates with another realistic software engineering experience.

2. Recent Developments

The current stage of development was initiated by another decision to convert to newer hardware. In 1988, after considerable debate, a lab based on Sun workstations was chosen. Because NSF assistance for this kind of activity virtually disappeared in the 80s, this equipment upgrade was predicated on University support. We had to decide between AT compatible machines, PS/2 machines, MacIntoshes, or Unix workstations. Since we use Unix machines throughout the upper division courses, it was decided to move the lower division courses to the same environment. There were some disadvantages to this approach, notably the lack of exposure to a variety of operating systems, however, the economies of scale coupled with the low price of powerful, multiuser Sun workstations dictated this change. Our hardware and software maintenance situation has been greatly simplified by this choice.

Since our Suns are all networked with EtherNet, we elected initially to use the low priced, diskless Sun 3/50's and 3/60's. This network used file servers and shared valuable resources, such as printers (particularly laser printers). When operating with individual PCs using floppy disks, we had considerable problems with software version control. The use of NFS with centralized file servers on a network has solved this problem. Networking also allows for mail, bulletin boards, easy software transfer, and many other benefits. When our network exceeded fifteen machines, the performance begin to degrade noticeably, primarily due to excessive swapping. Now that we have over twenty Sun workstations, we have had to address this performance problem. We have put a SCSI disk drive on selected workstations and upgraded RAM memory from 4 MB to 8 MB on all workstations We have also increased the RAM memory cn the file servers, so that we now have one server with 16 MB and three with 12 MB. These changes have resulted in 40% to 50% less swapping and significant performance increases. The fact that our network is not segmented has resulted in a lack of robustness - when the network goes down everyone is affected. As funds become available, we plan to establish a local network segment for each of our four file servers and its clients using filter repeaters between the segments. With our current equipment this would put four or five Suns on each segment.

Table 1 summarizes the hardware and software currently used in our programming courses.

Programming Course	Language(s)	Equipment
Introduction to Programming	Modula-2	Sun workstations
Intro. to Data Structures	Modula-2	Sun workstations
Assembly Lang./Machine Org.	Macro 11	DEC Pro 325, Pro 350
Symbolic Computation	Lisp, Prolog	Sun workstations
Software Engineering	Modula-2 or Ada	Suns or Sequent
Data Structures	Modula-2	Sun workstations
Programming Language Design I	Ada, Lisp, ML, Prolog, C++, Smalltalk	Sun workstations, Sequent
Operating Systems I	C	ATT 7300 Unix PC
Artificial Intelligence I	Lisp, Prolog	Sun workstations

Table 1 : Software & Hardware Used by Programming Courses

The last software conversion was based on the upgrade to Suns. Although the implementation language remained Modula-2, there was a major change in graphics support. Initially we moved the text-oriented components (the drills and programming quizzes) to the new environment using "curses", a non-bit-map text display system with simple windowing capability that runs on any ANSI-terminal emulation. We are currently developing a complete graphically-compatible package based on X11 software, an emerging defacto industry standard for bit-mapped windowing software. Once this is completed we will be able to move the tutorials.

Another problem we had to solve in our last conversion was proctor control of the lab environment. When working on stand-alone IBM PCs, this problem was largely mechanical: the proctors handed out and collected floppy disks as needed. Moving to an environment with networked, diskless workstations, an entirely different approach had to be developed. We developed a distributed communications system where a student running a menu program on one machine requests access to software (drills and p-quizzes) via a proctor program running on another machine.

In addition to moving the existing software to the Sun workstation environment, we have developed additional CAI materials to support instruction in abstract data types in our CS2 course [Kurtz 89]. Our past experiences in porting software between a variety of hardware and software systems convinced us that programming quizzes require remarkably little support software. Therefore, we developed two types of programming quizzes for our lower division data structures course. The first type of quiz provides an ADT and asks students to accomplish a particular task. For example, given an ADT for a stack of integers, the student must use only the operations provided to write a procedure that increments by one every item in the stack. The second type of programming quiz is to extend the functionality of an ADT by adding a new operation. In this case, the student must manipulate the actual representation of the ADT directly.

When we moved the introductory class to a Unix-based environment, we realized that some laboratory instruction would be needed for a small subset of Unix commands and for the GNU Emacs editor. For the first several weeks, a 90 minute lab session was offered to cover these basic commands. Students working at a console or terminal were led through a script of simple operations, including entry of a very small program in the editor, compiling, linking, and running the program. These orientation sessions were taught by the undergraduate lab manager. Although students were encouraged to go to one of these sessions, attendance was strictly voluntary. We soon found that this training was insufficient given the complexity of Unix and the complexity of the editor. Although manual pages are available on-line, this documentation was of little use for naive users.

We have instituted a policy of one hour per week scheduled lab time that is taught by the instructor. We have also switched to the vi editor for the introductory class. We provide a substantial lab manual written at a level appropriate for a new user [Reinfelds 89]. Except for the compilation commands, almost all instruction is on Unix itself. In other words, one fourth of our scheduled class time is currently being spent on instruction in the operating system and its associated software tools. This is a dramatic shift in emphasis from the early days of using PC's with DOS and a simple screen-oriented editor. Currently we are rather ambivalent about this shift in emphasis and feel that it remains to be seen if the shift is beneficial in the long run.

3. Speculation about Future Development

Because the recent hardware upgrade has brought us up to date with respect to instructional equipment, we can concentrate on determining the most appropriate directions for developing the courses supported by the lab and then acquiring/developing the necessary software. However, this will not be an easy task, owing to the large number of attractive directions for development. We visualize the possibilities as a tree of possible scenarios, with the root being our present position and two subtrees based on evolutionary and revolutionary developments, respectively. Of course a discrete representation of the possibilities is virtually impossible but Table 2 summarizes the possibilities that we find most attractive. These scenarios will also be affected by the general reorganization of the introductory CS courses as proposed by the Denning committee [Denning 89].

Evolutionary Scenarios
    Applied - CASE tools emphasis
    Formal - formal methodologies emphasis
    Intermediate - general tools with a formal basis
Revolutionary Scenarios
    Nonprocedural Paradigm - functional, object-oriented, logic programming
    Multi-Paradigm - procedural and nonprocedural

Table 2 : Possibilities for Instructional Development

Evolutionary Scenarios

In these scenarios, we envision extending our current approach to problem-solving and programming using procedural languages in the introductory sequence for CS majors. Some additional lab material, such as animated displays of algorithm execution [Brown

88], is virtually a *necessity*, regardless of the approach we take in different evolutionary scenarios. The NSF Workshop on Undergraduate Computer Science Education [NSF 88] clearly recommends such an approach.

What we call the applied approach would place increased emphasis on software engineering. Our current problem solving approach in CS1 is based on a simplified form of the traditional software engineering life cycle and we emphasize the use of general design techniques such as structure charts, modular design charts, information hiding and data abstraction. We do not anticipate a language change, because we feel quite satisfied with Modula-2 and find it easy to move students to Ada in the software engineering course. However, we could introduce a few CASE tools at the end of CS1 and the beginning of CS2 to increase the software engineering emphasis. Our choice of hardware permits this, and the tools could be chosen to be consistent with current course material. Additional CAI material might have to be developed, however. Also, the expense of obtaining the appropriate tools might be a problem, although it now seems possible to obtain reasonable tools at a bearable price [Sidbury 89]. Perhaps the renewed interest of NSF in supporting educational activities, and the current emphasis of the CISE Directorate of NSF on software capitalization would mitigate such problems even further. Nevertheless, we do not find this approach very appealing because:

1. No single CASE product is available for the entire spectrum of hardware and software environments [Long 89].
2. The evolutionary and extensibility capacities of CASE tools, and hence their long term significance is uncertain.
3. CASE tools certainly seem to speed program development, but the degree to which they help to develop problem solving skills is less clear.

What we call the formal approach would emphasize correctness of program development through formal techniques. Our current textual material emphasizes the use of assertions, but in a relatively informal way [Adams 88]. Our material is fairly consistent with more formal methodologies, such as the one proposed by Gries [Gries 81], but some modifications would be required and the development of some additional CAI material would be necessary. Also, some additions to Modula-2 would be very desirable. For example, in an earlier development we added an assertional checking and symbolic execution facility to UCSD Pascal and this facility could readily be adapted to Modula-2.

The applied and formal approaches are not, strictly speaking, mutually exclusive and our current approach could be considered as a balance between these two extremes. The intermediate approach mentioned in Table 2 would perhaps be more consistent with this balance. UNIX, which we presently use on the Suns, can be considered to be a general and more conceptual CASE environment than commercial CASE products [Mynatt 89]. Thus we might could realize some of the advantages of the applied approach, without suffering the disadvantages, by devoting more time in our introductory sequence to the use of appropriate UNIX systems programs. The lack of a conceptual framework is a disadvantage of this possibility, however. An interesting possibility that provides a conceptual framework is the programmer's apprentice [Rich 88], which is based on a software assistant with a substantial knowledge of programming techniques and a powerful reasoning facility. Unfortunately, only a prototype called KBEmacs (knowledge-based editor in Emacs) has been developed, but the potential of this approach might make it wise to undertake or participate in the development of such a system.

Revolutionary Scenarios

This is much more speculative because it is based on a more fundamental change in our approach to the introductory sequence for CS majors. In this scenario, we would place much more emphasis on problem solving and, in particular, we would attempt to broaden the traditional view of solving problems through the development of procedural algorithms that are developed with sequential execution in mind. The approach is based on the hypothesis that this traditional view of solving problems with computers may be narrow and limiting within the next decade. To attain a broader less limiting view will require the use of design/analysis techniques and programming languages more conducive to thinking about the development of nonprocedural algorithms involving parallel execution. Such techniques and languages will be based on models of computation involving a higher level of abstraction than the traditional procedural (von Neumann style). For example, far less programmer description of the order of evaluation would be necessary. Because nonprocedural models of computation are usually expressed in functional languages [Skillicorn 89], the functional programming paradigm is one obvious candidate. The logic programming and object-oriented paradigms are almost equally as obvious and each has strong adherents within our department. In fact, we have just introduced a junior level course in symbolic computation (using Lisp and Prolog) that is a prerequisite for our senior level AI course, and we also expose students to object-oriented programming languages, such as Smalltalk or C++. However, this is all at the upper division and several faculty members feel strongly that their favorite paradigm should be the basis for the programming aspect of the curriculum and hence the primary topic of CS1. Others feel that this approach would be throwing the baby out with the bath water, in discarding a valuable and proven procedural paradigm, and that one limiting point of view would be replaced by another less limiting but still too narrow point of view. Also, the dramatic nature of this change would make it difficult to implement.

An alternative to the single paradigm approach is the multiparadigm approach that would promote using the appropriate paradigm for each aspect of a system for which it is best suited [Zave 89]. In this approach, the functional, object-oriented, and logical paradigms would be introduced much earlier in the curriculum, along with the traditional procedural paradigm. This would be a dramatic change in the curriculum, but not as dramatic as the change to a single nonprocedural paradigm, in that the procedural paradigm would still be taught, albeit as one of several possibilities rather than the only possibility. Thus other courses could be changed more gradually and with greater care. Perhaps the most difficult problems with this approach is the need for a unifying concept for multiparadigm programming and the related problem of the need for a means for paradigm composition [Wells 89]. Nondeterminism has been proposed as a possibility for composing paradigms [Zave 89] and it could provide a unifying concept, if one views nondeterminism as parallelism at a higher level of abstraction. We think this is a very attractive possibility, but one that requires more research in paradigm composition and in refining a pedagogical approach based on nondeterminnism.

Obviously, a single nonprocedural paradigm or multiparadigm approach would mean discarding our current approach along with all of our current CAI software. Clearly this is not a step to be taken lightly and probably not to be taken at all unless substantial external support could be obtained. Nevertheless, some feel that the traditional approach is fundamentally too narrow and limiting, and the longer the delay in breaking from this approach, the more traumatic and difficult the break will be. A strategy that we find attractive, is to pursue the intermediate evolutionary scenario in the short term leading to the multiparadigm scenario in the long run.

4. Summary

We have chronicled the development of our undergraduate laboratory over the past decade, emphasizing the beneficial software engineering side effects for our undergraduate staff. The effort to maintain the lab at the state-of-the-art, with respect to both hardware/software and pedagogical developments, has been considerable. Unfortunately, or fortunately depending on your point of view, the effort to maintain a state-of-the-art lab in the next few years promises to be even greater, as the two scenarios described above indicate. Our past development would have been impossible without informal cooperation with other institutions, notably UCSD and UC Irvine. Perhaps more formal arrangements with many institutions will be needed for future developments, particularly if the multiparadigm scenario is to be pursued effectively.

Bibliography

[Adams 88] J. Adams, P. Gabrini, B. Kurtz, **An Introduction to Computer Science with Modula-2**, D. C. Heath, Lexington, MA, 1988

[Adams 83] J. Adams, M. Landis, A Computer Based Tutorial on Mathematical Induction, *Proc. of the National Educational Computing Conference*, 1983

[Adams 81] J. Adams, B. MacKichan, R. Hunter, Starting a Computer Based Learning Project, *Proc. of the National Educational Computing Conference*, June 1981

[Bowles 78] K. Bowles, A CS1 Course Based on Stand-Alone Microcomputers, *Proceedings of the Ninth Technical Symposium on Computer Science Education*, Detroit, February 1978, pp. 125-127

[Brown 88] M. Brown, Exploring Algorithms Using Balsa-II, *IEEE Computer*, Vol. 21, No. 5, pp. 14-36, May 1988

[Denning 89] P. Denning, et.al., Computing as a Discipline, *CACM*, 32:1 (January 1989), pp. 9-23

[Gries 81] D. Gries, **The Science of Programming**, New York, Springer-Verlag, 1981.

[Kurtz 89] B. Kurtz, H. Pfeiffer, Developing Programming Quizzes to Support Instruction in Abstract Data Types, *SIGCSE Bulletin*, 21:1 (February 1989), pp. 66-70

[Long 89] J. Long, CASE at Texas Instruments, *Texas Instruments Technical Journal*, v. 6, no. 5, Set.-Oct. 1989.

[Mynatt 89] B. T. Mynatt and M. Leventhal, A CASE Primer for Computer Science Educators, *SIGCSE Bulletin*, v. 21, no. 1, Feb. 1989.

[NSF 88] Undergraduate Computer Science Education, Report on a Workshop Sponsered by the NSF, James Foley, Editor, The George Washington University, March 10-11, 1988

[Reinfelds 89] J. Reinfelds, *CS271 Laboratory Manual*, Computer Science Department, New Mexico State University, 1989

[Rich 89] C. Rich and R. C. Waters, The Programmer's Apprentice: A Research Overview, *IEEE Computer*, Sept. 89.

[Sidbury 89] J. R. Sidbury, R. Plishka, and J. Beidler, CASE and the Undergraduate Curriculum, *SIGCSE Bulletin*, v. 21, no. 1, Feb. 1989.

[Skillicorn 89] D. B. Skillicorn, A Taxonomy for Computer Architectures, *IEEE Computer*, Sept. 89.

[Volper, in print] D. Volper, S. Franklin, Computer aided instruction in a large introductory computer science course for CS majors, accepted by *Education and Computing*

[Wells 89] M. B. Wells and B. Kurtz, Teaching Multiple Programming Paradigms: A Proposal for a Paradigm-General Pseudocode, *SIGCSE Bulletin*, 21:1 (February 1989), pp. 246-251

[Zave 89] P. Zave, A Compositional Approach to Multiparadigm Programming, *IEEE Software*, Sept. 89.

-- StarLite --
A Software Education Laboratory

Robert P. Cook
Lifeng Hsu
Department of Computer Science
University of Virginia
Charlottesville, VA 22903

Abstract. *Laboratories are a prerequisite to all scientific investigation. The ability to quickly create experiments amplifies a scientist's intellectual ability. For education, students experiment to learn and to gain experience. Ideally, a laboratory helps a student visualize a problem domain, such as concurrent or distributed systems. Eventually, the students learn to reason about a problem domain abstractly, but typically the experience must come first.*

1.0   Introduction

Software support for distributed programming lags far behind hardware development because of the complexity of the area and the lack of tools. In the past, to experiment with software for distributed or multiprocessor systems, a systems researcher had to purchase multiple CPUs and network interfaces. Such an investment is impractical for many people. Furthermore, even for those with network access, tools for conducting research on software systems for parallel and distributed system are minimal. Now, with the StarLite environment, only a single computer is required.

StarLite supports the development of distributed software on a single computer by isolating the machine-dependent portions of a software system using modular programming techniques to provide machine-independent interfaces that can be manipulated to simulate the behavior of the target hardware. Each device in the StarLite environment is presented to the user as an abstract data type. For instance, a Modula-2 *definition* module is used to represent the test software's view of a machine model, while a Modula-2 *implementation* module emulates the characteristics of physical machines and devices.

The StarLite environment currently supports four research areas: *programming environments, operating systems, database,* and *computer network* technology. The environment includes a Modula-2 compiler, an interpreter, a window package, a viewer, and an optional simulation package. The compiler and interpreter are implemented in C for portability. The rest of the software is in Modula-2. The system currently runs on SUN workstations and PCs.

We are currently teaching a distributed operating systems course that uses StarLite. The course is based on domain analysis and interface design as the foundation for an investigation of implementation options. It is open to upper level undergraduate and graduate students. The course load depends on each student's interest and background. The basis of study is a UNIX variant, Phoenix, that we are developing using StarLite. Since the C code for the compiler and interpreter are irrelevant to the course, only the StarLite components written in Modula-2 are presented to the class.

We emphasize the following general themes throughout the course:

o   Selection and utilization of appropriate tools
o   Modular decomposition
o   Software reuse
o   Layered interfaces
o   Open architecture

The general requirements are as follows:

o   Study problems of software development.
o   Construct parallel and distributed programs by individual effort using StarLite's concurrent and distributed programming kernels.
o   Construct a small-scale distributed operating system and use StarLite tools to debug the system and to analyze the performance of the program.
o   Present the project. This includes documentation and evaluation.

2.0 Approaches and Tools

This section discusses our pedagogical approach and the tools used in the course. The discussion is divided into the following four parts:

1. Methodology: Some of the present operating system design philosophies are described.

2. Programming and Tools: This section describes the students' programming exercises and the StarLite tools.

3. Observations: Some observations from past experiments are presented.

4. Examples: Some examples of the use of StarLite for multi-processor and distributed systems are presented.

2.1 Methodology

In addition to various Operating System topics, the basic problems and concepts of software development are introduced. Also, operating system design philosophies and the StarLite tools are discussed. The students are normally given questions before class for discussion. Typical questions include: How many ways are there to implement an abstract data type? How often do the students code the same algorithms for different applications? How can object-based programming paradigms affect operating system design? These questions lead into to a discussion of techniques for modular decomposition with an emphasis on software reuse. Other questions are chosen from paging, resource allocation, and file system design.

2.1.1 Modular decomposition and software reuse

The current problems in software education come from many sources. First, according to Liskov[1], of the three kinds of abstractions -- procedural, control, and data abstractions-- only procedural abstraction is supported well by conventional languages which, unfortunately, still dominate most of our educational environments. Secondly, our pedagogical approaches have long been focused on *problems of implementation* rather than *problems of specification*, while the later often turn out to be more fundamental in the long run. Finally, even if specification is stressed, operational specifications[2] rather than abstract specifications are still the major theme of many software design courses. Thus, the common dilemma of higher-level software courses is that the students almost always end up decomposing the *program* instead of the *problem*. Therefore, for every application and problem, we challenge the students to construct interfaces that could potentially last forever rather than writing programs just to solve the problem as given.

2.1.2 Layered interfaces

Generally there are two design options to choose from as the basis for an interface standard: *flat* and *layered*. A system with a flat interface, such as UNIX operating system, is essentially closed; that is none of the interfaces used in the implementation can be accessed. Flat interfaces are inflexible and typically trade performance and control for generality. A layered interface specification, such as the ISO OSI definition[3] for network protocols, overcomes the deficiencies of the traditional, flat operating system interface designs by allowing the application engineer to choose an interface layer that most closely fits the problem to be solved.

Another advantage of a layered design is that layers can be omitted to save space. For example, if an application does not use files, the file system could be omitted. It is also possible to implement layers in hardware to improve performance.

More importantly, by using the layered approach, the design and implementation of the system is simplified. As a result, clean and lucid user interfaces are easier to construct, and the system is much more amenable to investigation and experimentation.

2.1.3 Open architecture

StarLite is designed to support an arbitrary number of different, validated implementations for a given interface. As a result, the system as a whole is designed as an *open* systems architecture that can be tuned to meet application requirements. Examples of different implementation options that can be used with the same interface specification include CPU and disk scheduling algorithms or hierarchical versus flat-file name interpretation.

The long-term goal of the StarLite project is to create a system generator that could automatically select implementations from a module library based on specified application requirements and a given target architecture. The first step toward achieving this goal is to create a library of implementation modules suitable for mission critical applications. The orientation of the class is concerned with creating such a library.

2.2 Programming and Tools

We believe that a fundamental understanding of concurrent programming concepts is essential to constructing a correct and efficient operating system. Each student, therefore, is required to construct parallel and distributed programs using the StarLite concurrent and distributed programming kernels. The implementations of the *coroutine* and *process* abstractions, as well as various synchronization and interprocess communication models[4], are studied in great detail.

Students are also required to experiment with StarLite tools such as the Viewer and Profiler. The StarLite Viewer subsumes the functionality of a traditional debugger, but is quite a bit more. First, the Viewer allows the user to explore, monitor and modify any thread, module, procedure, or variable on any processor. Also, all hardware details are accessible from the viewer. An example of the Viewer is given in Figure 1.

Figure 1 illustrates a program, TreeDemo, that creates a binary tree of letter-number pairs. The display contains Source, Coroutine, Module, Message, Control and Data windows. A break point has been set in the source at line 46. This is denoted in the Source window by bold text. The Coroutine window lists the content of the hardware registers as well as the procedure call chain. Break points are also listed in the Control window. The Module window lists the module names for the components of a program.

The Data window lists the name, type, and value for the variables in the procedure or module that has been selected with the mouse. The Viewer allows a user to dynamically attach a filter to any type name. In Figure 1, when the variable "tree" was selected, its data structure was made available to a filter that displayed it in graphic form.

Filters can be easily defined by users to provide application-specific views of data. The figure also illustrates the interaction that is possible between a filter and the Viewer. For example, the node labeled "m" was selected with the mouse. As a result, the Data window was updated to display the data item for node "m".

Figure 2 depicts the StarLite Profiler. The user may monitor the execution of a system by inspecting the frequency distribution charts. The different charts include frequency distributions of where the system is spending its time by module number, where selected modules are spending their time by program counter values, and op code usage in the architecture. With the aid of the Profiler, hot spots in the program can be easily detected and then the user can tune the code to improve system performance.

In Figure 2, we are profiling an arbitrary-precision integer module while it is computing 23 raised to the 239th power. By selecting the "arbitrary" entry in the Module Key window, the program counter chart for that module is displayed. By selecting the highest spike in the Program Counter chart, the corresponding position in the source text is displayed. In this case, it is the PowerInt procedure.

Finally, each student is expected to do a semester project. Since the system is *open*, a student may either evaluate alternative implementations for existing interfaces, or construct additional layers of software.

2.3 Observations

StarLite is based on a layered design with standard interfaces. Two of the research issues are how to partition the layers and how to define the interfaces at each layer.

To experiment with different options, the class designed and implemented a UNIX-compatible operating system according to the layering principles defined by ISO[3]. The StarLite UNIX is proprietary in that it is not based upon, nor does it contain, any code from other UNIX implementations. We, including the students in the past, have rewritten the system several times to try different layering and implementation strategies. We have found interface specification to be a more demanding task than doing the implementation. In other words, writing a monolithic piece of code to solve a problem is much easier than creating a layered design in which the layers are intended to form functionally complete and useful subsets that have a lifetime beyond the program in which they are contained.

We have also found two other problems with the layered design. The first problem is the overhead of procedure calls through multiple layers of software. The second problem results from application requirements, such as protection features, which can affect interfaces and implementations at a number of layers. Even if the requirement is removed at a higher layer, there may be unused procedures and data structures at lower layers that affect performance. Both problems are being solved by improving compiler technology.

2.4 Examples

2.4.1 StarLite machine models

The StarLite interpreter supports the simultaneous execution of multiple virtual processors in a single address space. Figure 3 describes the three virtual machine models supported by StarLite: single processor, multiprocessor, and distributed processors. All software developed in the laboratory uses one of these machine models as a base. For distributed processors, each virtual processor has its own copy of the test software. For the other machine models, the software is shared by all processors.

2.4.2 Multiprocessor machine models

Figure 4 illustrates the Phoenix operating system running on a sixteen-node multiprocessor system. It also contains a visualization aid that depicts the state of each processor. Each small box indicates the current state of an individual processor. The letter R stands for Running, and I for Idle. The example shows that only two processors are being utilized.

Figure 5 shows several of the StarLite visualization abstract data types: *state queue, visual disks* and *clocks*. In the *state queue* data type, the shaded area in each square indicates a frequency count for a single simulation entity. This visualization aid is particularly useful for spotting system bottlenecks, such as long delay lines for queues. The letter 'V' in the disk window indicates the current position of the read/write head over the surface of the disk. The numbered positions represent cylinders and the rows represent disk surfaces.

2.4.3 Distributed system models

Figure 6 illustrates the user view of a 4-node network. Each node has a window that represents its console. Furthermore, each node is running the Phoenix operating system developed by the class. Two of the nodes have booted up to the shell level and are ready to accept user commands. One of the nodes has tracing enabled for its disk actions. After the nodes have booted, the StarLite user can execute system tests, collect statistics, or examine/modify the system state.

The Control Panel window allows the user to control the state of each network processor. By using the FAIL and REBOOT options, the student may crash and reboot nodes and then observe the network performance or fault-tolerance of their algorithms. The FAIL SOFT option generates a power fail interrupt on the selected processor. The PATTERN option is used to fail and reboot processors under program control.

2.4.4 Ethernet model

StarLite also includes windows for EtherNets. As operators, such as "read" or "write," are applied to the simulated devices, the effects are depicted in their windows. For a network device, the network state as well as each packet's size and destination address are displayed. Optionally, the transferred data can also be listed. Each EtherNet window represents a network of as many as several hundred stations. The state of each station is denoted by a letter, with upper case indicating a pending request, and lower case a completed operation. For example, a transmit request remains pending until either the backoff algorithm fails or the transmission completes.

The EtherNet operators are Transmit, Broadcast, Receive, and receive-All. There is also an Idle state. The standard menu options are *Break, Continue, Speed, Examine, Stop,* and *Exit*. The *Speed* option is particularly useful because it can be used to vary the speed of a physical device so that experiments can be run with different configurations of networks and disks. By increasing the speed of one component we may expose bottlenecks in others.

3.0 Conclusion

StarLite is an effective software education tool. It is the only realistic alternative for students who do not have access to a distributed system. StarLite forces the user to concentrate on the important aspects of a problem by eliminating concern over details. By encouraging the study of elegant and efficient interfaces, the students learn a more disciplined approach to distributed systems development.

References

[1]   Liskov, B. et al, Abstraction Mechanisms in CLU. *CACM 20*, 8(Aug 1977), 564-576.

[2]   Wegner, P., Programming Languages--Concepts and Research Directions, *Research Directions in Software Technology*, MIT Press, Edited by P. Wegner, (1979) 425-489.

[3]   Zimmermann, H., OSI reference Model--The ISO Model of Architecture for Open Systems Interconnection, *IEEE Transactions on Communications COM-28*, (April 1980) 425-432.

[4]   Cook, R.P., StarMod, A Language for Distributed Programming, reprinted in *Concurrent programming*, Addison-Wesley, edited by N. Gehani and A.D. McGettrick, (1988).

104

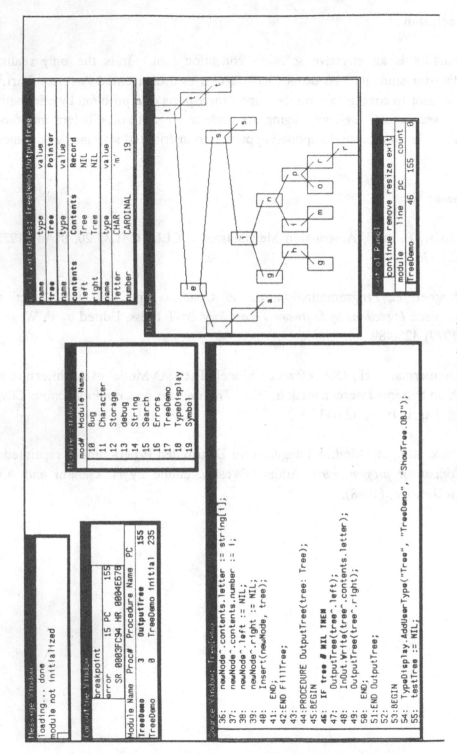

Figure 1. The StarLite Viewer

105

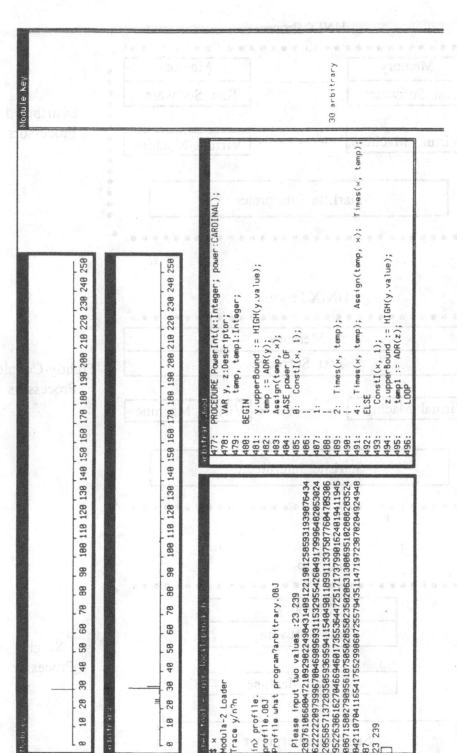

Figure 2. The StarLite Profiler

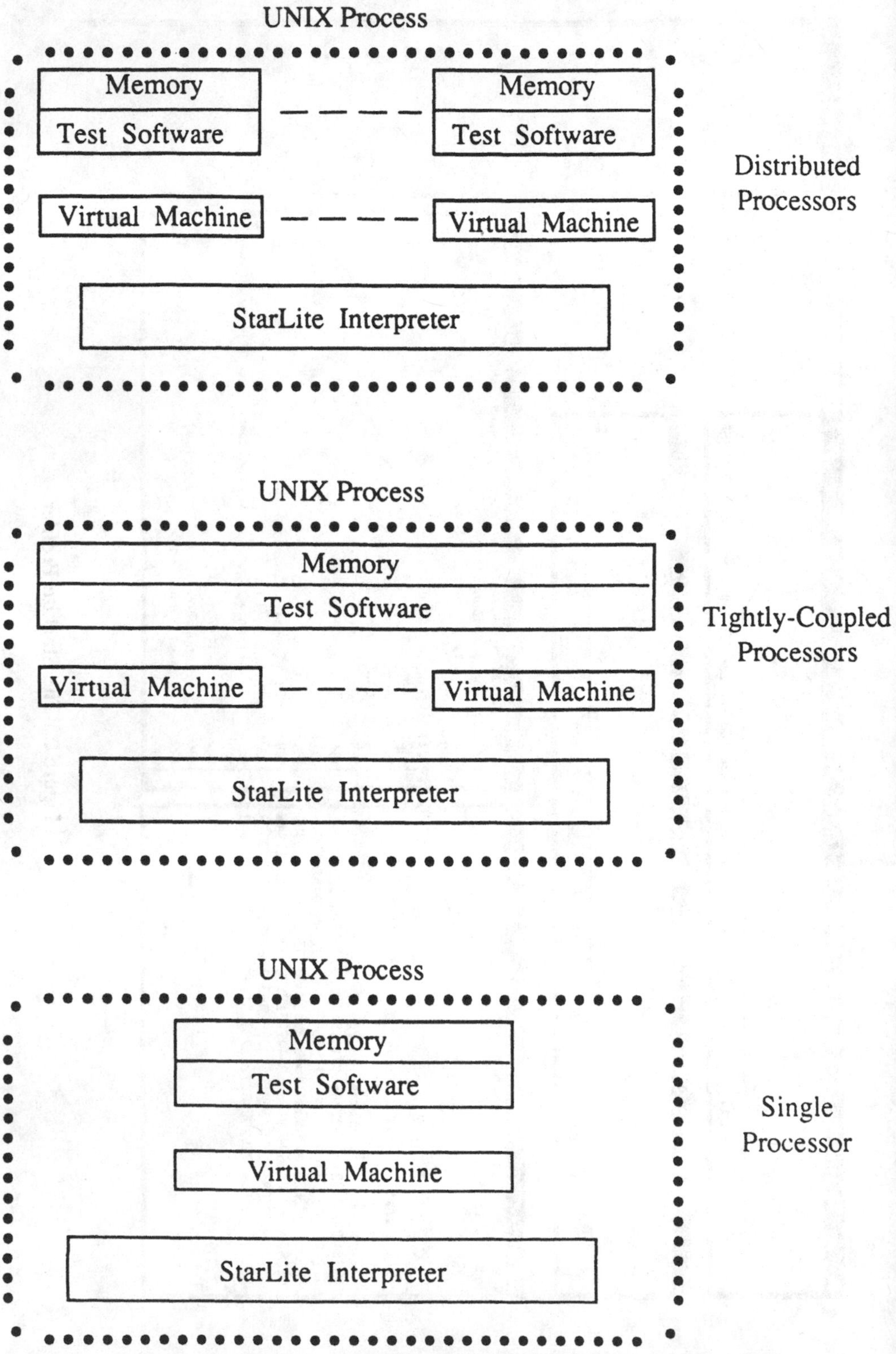
UNIX Process
Memory
Test Software
Memory
Test Software
Virtual Machine
Virtual Machine
StarLite Interpreter
Distributed Processors
UNIX Process
Memory
Test Software
Virtual Machine
Virtual Machine
StarLite Interpreter
Tightly-Coupled Processors
UNIX Process
Memory
Test Software
Virtual Machine
StarLite Interpreter
Single Processor

Figure 3. StarLite Machine Models

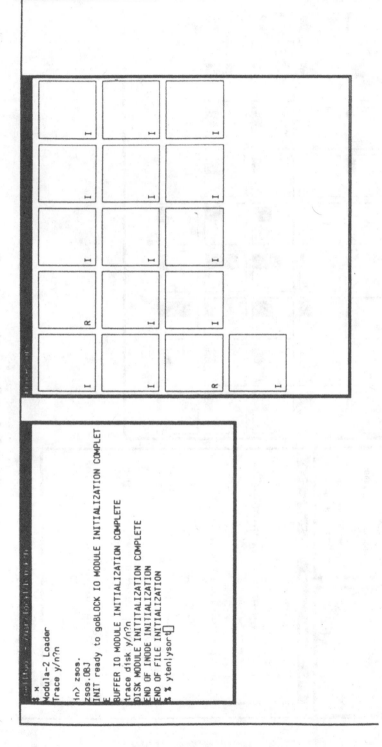

Figure 4. The Multiprocessor Window

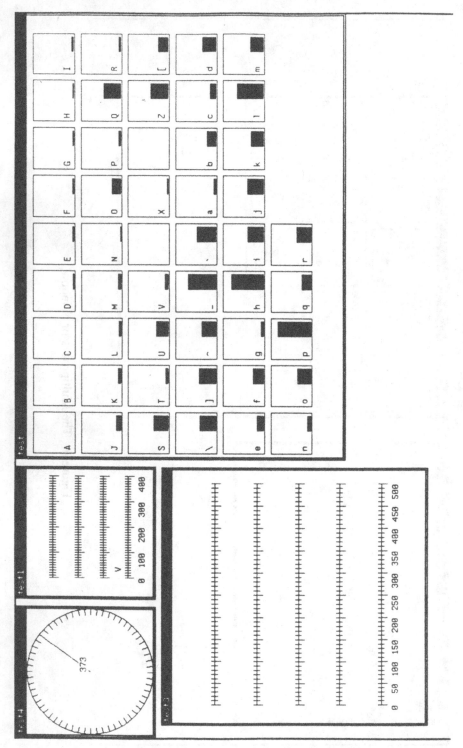

Figure 5. Visualization Abstract Data Types

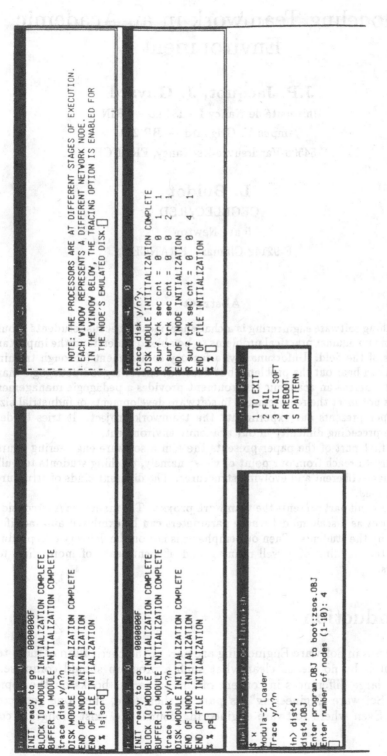

Figure 6. A 4-Node Distributed System

Modeling Teamwork in an Academic Environment

J.P. Jacquot, J. Guyard

Université de Nancy I – ISIAL – CRIN

Campus V. Grignard — BP 239

F-54506 Vandœuvre-lès-Nancy, FRANCE

L. Boidot

CEGELEC/RED

5 av. Newton

F-92142 Clamart, FRANCE

Abstract

Teaching software engineering is a challenge, mostly because students should have come up against practical problems to be able to understand the important concepts of the field. Unfortunately, a factory environment (through training courses) can bear out the problems but does not ensure a good pedagogic management whereas an academic environment provides a pedagogic management but does not meet the requirements in software developments of industrial size. This paper presents our experiment: the teamwork project. It tries to deal with the preceding difficulty in our academic environment.

The first part of the paper presents the aim a software engineering course should try to reach from our point of view: namely, teaching students to build and manage coherent and evolving structures. The different kinds of structures are discussed.

The second part presents the teamwork project. The main idea is to consider this project as a scale model whose parameters can be exhibited and modified actively by the students. Then our emphasis is not on the delivery of a product but on the building of a well-running and efficient team of more than ten members.

1 Introduction

Although courses in Software Engineering are part of the curriculum of most technical universities, it is by no means clear what such a program should comprise. If one considers the large differences in content of the numerous books on the topic, all of which have "Software Engineering" as part of their title, then one gets convinced of this fact. Even where software engineering courses do exist alongside computer science courses, they have often been created for the sake of fashion or for a short-term industrial need, rather than as a necessary complement for a full education. Sometimes the software engineering curriculum is no more than a very good computer science curriculum.

The confusion between software engineering and computer science arises from their closeness, partly due to their infancy. The comparison with other engineering-type activities – electronic for instance – clearly shows that rigorous foundations exist for engineering sciences. Moreover their industrial character relies on better established techniques.

The problem could be stated that way: "Can software engineering be taught?" Wasserman [WF76] answered the question in this way:

- Any software engineering student must bear in mind the fact that he has to link computer science principles with the use of tools and methods (including management techniques)

- Many concepts of software engineering can be explained through lectures and reading, but these have to be put into practice, wherein the students would "get their hands dirty".

In short, teaching software engineering seems rather difficult nowadays as it looks more like a craft to be learned than an academic subject to be taught.

Till recently, students have developed medium sized projects without team organization. Nevertheless, this generally works because they can solve the interface problem by mutual agreement, due to the small size of the team — two or three people. Real integration problems can be understood only by simulating real project development [HW77], [Wor87], [Tom89], [Kin89]. However, teamwork problems are as fundamental here as in the other branches of engineering, but due to the totally intellectual character of software, the organization of team and the dividing up of work are not standardized and vary from project to project. One of the main reasons is that the structure of the team will be conditioned by the architecture of the product, this last one being unknown at the beginning of the project. As a consequence the team and its components must be ready to evolve in a dynamic – but organized – way during the progress of the project.

The actual and concrete problem is then the following: How far can we go in the university curriculum to get as close as possible to the real world? Is it worthwhile to make the student work as a professional by simulating, as best we can, work in a team, pointing out communication problems and task allotment which are the keys to a successful project? Is it not more realistic to let the students discover these problems by themselves when they start working with companies? We think the answer to this last question is no. If a young professional has only academic background, his technical skill, excellent thought it may be, will probably be impaired if he finds himself overwhelmed by the adaptation to organization and teamwork. Then, due to this partial waste of time, the student's academic knowledge will be weakened before it gets to the professional community. In this case global technology transfer and evolution of the profession will suffer.

Having recognized the need, we want to show in this paper our efforts to solve the problem. We have followed our fundamental pedagogic assumption: "one learns only what one needs". The key point in our teaching approach is to convince our students that in their professional life they will quickly need to show their capacity for structuring if they wish to be regarded as engineers. In the first section we will briefly present our graduate curriculum in software engineering. Then we present the different structuring components of the software engineering activity. In the third section we describe the actual teamwork experiment. Finally we give our observations and the early conclusions we have drawn and what we expect to improve for next year's experiment.

2 Overview of the curriculum

The "DESS (Diplôme d'Etudes Scientifiques Supérieures) en Génie Logiciel" is the French equivalent of a Masters degree in Software Engineering. Its objectives are to provide professional graduate education together with a curriculum which meets the demands of industrial software development and management. It requires a one-year school attendance. The class size is about 15 students (13 in the 88/89 year). Students are from several backgrounds, but they all have two years undergraduate education in computer science. They also have solid grounding in Mathematics. The academic year lasts only six months, the remaining four months are dedicated to a training course in a firm. During these six months, the students spend a third of their time taking general courses on marketing, English (remember we are French!) and complementary courses on advanced aspects of computer science. The rest of the curriculum is devoted to software engineering topics, fundamental as well as applied. This specific course is divided into four themes, each of them being realized by two or three modules: foundations of software engineering, advanced programming techniques, tools and environment and software production.

As a general rule, each course is concluded by a short programming assignment to stress the practical capabilities of the students. One of these assignments is upgraded to the scale of a project in which the students have to cope with the reality of professional teamwork. This paper presents this particular project and the fundamental pedagogic importance it has gained in the curriculum.

3 Are you sure you teach Software Engineering?

The provocative title of this section reminds us that teaching any engineering activity remains a pedagogical challenge. The teaching of traditional engineering, e.g. civil, mechanical, aeronautics or electrical for instance, has sufficient history so that the curricula are well defined, the tools to be presented are identified and the effective pedagogical strategies are arguably reasonably well known. All this experience provides us with some directions on how to build a software engineering course, but, due to the very nature of software as a technical object, we cannot simply copy a successful course. In this section, we present the difference between software and other engineering and we then try to analyze the specific difficulties.

In traditional engineering fields, the final product results from the integration of very different material objects. Each of these objects is clearly identified by its main function, its relation with other objects and the craftmanship with which it is associated. At the project level, all these objects are given from the beginning (at least in a generic way: in a plane, the engine is a mandatory component, even if the actual engine of the final plane does not exist at the beginning of the project). The engineering problem is then to integrate several objects and to coordinate several types of craftmanship. As a consequence, the engineer must have a technical culture broad enough to encompass all the different kinds of knowledge, the specific constraints and mutual interactions. But, this is compensated by the fact that the obvious structure of the product implies the actual structure of the project.

By way of contrast, in a software engineering project, there seems to be only one object: the software. This has the advantage of lowering the cultural requirements. But, as a drawback, the engineer must reinvent, at the beginning of each new project, a structure *ab initio*. This structuring activity is far from easy, particularly since it involves very different kinds of structures: software structure, activity structure, time structure, team structure, ...

Our pedagogical goal is then to teach the students how to design and justify these structures. A general starting point in this type of teaching is to show the need of the structures by analyzing previous either successful or failed projects. Unfortunately, software engineering is too young an activity to provide us with a good corpus of fully described examples. So, we must find a means of convincing the students. Our previous experience has shown that to convince students of this particular need is akin to the activity of jumping hurdles. Let us see the hurdles, classified by the type of structuring.

3.1 Team structuring

The three prominent characteristics of a professional team are foreign to the average student:

1. *the hierarchy*. Running a successful team requires it has a coherent organization, which, in turn, implies some kind of hierarchy. Generally, students try to avoid building hierarchical structures, as for example the Chief Programmer Team [MB73]. One of the main reasons lies in the students' concept of the class as a coherent group of peers. Thus they are afraid to break their unity by distinguishing anyone among them and they resent a negative judgement on a result as being a judgement on their own person, not on their own work.

2. *the rigid communication channels*. Beyond a team size of five, the combinatorial complexity of the natural communication network becomes very hard to manage. Efficiency requires that formal communication channels should be defined. In practice, this means that meetings with a chairman must be scheduled, that written activity reports must be furnished to the project manager, that written documents must be standardized, and so on. Our students are unaware of these communication problems. The main reason lies in their previous experience with program development in which they worked in small teams (2 or 4 participants). Since these previous developments were successful (otherwise, they would not have got their degrees), they tend to reuse the same organization scheme.

3. *the specialization of the tasks.* Although the idea of defining and allotting individual tasks is accepted, we have noted that the realization of this idea raises some difficulties. A first one is the feeling that anyone who is assigned a technical task will learn less than one who is assigned a functional task (quality control or project secretary for instance). A second difficulty is tied to the scale of values implicitly associated with the activities; everybody wants to make the general design but nobody wants to write the user's manual.

With regard to the inter-personal structuring, we can sum up our pedagogical goal as providing each student with the ability to place himself clearly into the team as a professional and not as an individual.

3.2   Documents structuring

A piece of software involves a huge quantity of documents among which the program proper is only one small part. During their previous curriculum, the students have been presented with the different types of documents: requirements, formal specifications, functional design, detailed design, user's documentation, program text, and so on. Each document corresponds to an activity which has been studied in a dedicated course. Thus, the students have been provided with the methods and techniques related to each activity and the related skills have been developed with specific assignments. Nevertheless, we constantly notice that the students have a lot of difficulties in writing documents which are legible, clearly distinct from one to another, and well aimed, when they are confronted with a complete project.

Our first attempt to solve this problem was to give lectures about the standardized document plans issued by the IEEE or the AFNOR[1] for example; this failed partly because the documents had a good skeleton but bad flesh! Actually, these disappointing results show two very interesting facts: the aim of a document can be understood only after some real experience, the dividing line between the different documents cannot be defined abstractedly for each and every software project. For instance, the point where the specification ends and the functional design begins must be specifically defined within each project. In fact, structuring the documentation of a project is a creative work which cannot be reduced to the mere instantiation of a general frame.

With regard to the documents, our pedagogical aim is to trigger the particular kind of creativity they require, and show its necessity.

3.3   Time structuring

The delivery of software on time requires that tools such as cost predictive models and project management techniques should be used by the team. Our problem is then to urge the students to use effectively and as a matter of routine such tools for their project.

One might think, and we did think this at the time, that their previous experience might have shown them this necessity. Unfortunately, this seems a false assumption.

---

[1]French standards association

From our point of view, the problem is inherent to the academic curriculum. A typical academic assignment is aimed at exemplifying a particular concept of computer science. Thus, it is totally defined and scaled by the teaching team which gives it to the students according to their capacities and work load. From the students side, this means that they get a precise problem statement and an imperative deadline, none of them being subject to negotiation. Should the problem be badly stated or badly scaled (by grossly underestimating the size of code for instance), the project will be a failure. The interesting thing to note is that, in such a bad case the student is not responsible for the failure. So, the students have the conception that the time organization of a software development is an external parameter which lies out of their reach. Our primary aim is to reverse this conception and to make the students feel fully responsible for the time management of their project.

With regard to time, our pedagogical aim is to introduce this parameter as an internal variable of a project by making each member of the team as the whole team responsible for it.

3.4 Program structuring

When the students enter the software engineering course, they already have a significant amount of programming behind them. They have been taught the state-of-the-art methods of analyzing and programming, and they know how to use them on "small" programs. As a result they are able, given an assignment, to produce a program with soundly structured components. Nevertheless our experience shows that they have a great deal of difficulty in using their structuring capacity when the size of the project increases.

From our point of view, the problem is due to the path they followed designing the structure in their previous developments. The most common way is to define a general, flexible structure and then to refine and make it rigid. Roughly speaking, the program structure is then a result, not a starting point, of the development. In fact, this kind of development technique corresponds exactly to the activity of prototyping. A typical student would only have been required to develop prototypes, never to develop an operational piece of software.

We must stress the fact that the "prototype bias" cannot be removed during the earlier student curriculum. Each assignment is a discovery, for the students, of how a concept is implemented or used; the students' mistakes are part of the learning process. Another point to note is that the students were in a good position for prototype development. They worked in small teams where everyone knows everything in the program; then, modifying a component or its interface is a simple task.

Clearly, the development of an operational piece of software is organized the other way round: the components and their interfaces must be totally defined *a priori* and, as far as possible, never redefined. This structuring activity requires that the software should be considered from a very abstract point of view while deliberately ignoring the implementation details. Such a capacity can be acquired only from wide professional experience. Our pedagogical aim is then to stress the fundamental importance of this capacity and to involve the students in a real case study which can be freely criticized.

3.5 Concluding remarks

As we have pointed out earlier, we do not consider the transmission of technical knowledge as our main pedagogical problem. This is not to say that this part of the software engineering course is unnecessary. In fact, the academic environment was specifically designed for this kind of teaching. The observation of our students during their first employment clearly indicates that they are at the top of their art and have been provided with the technical knowledge necessary to work in any high tech environment.

The pedagogical challenge is to make the students pass smoothly from an academic way of working to a professional way of working. The most striking difference between the two worlds can be summed up in one word: *size*. The preceding points show the most apparent impacts of this change in scale.

Different strategies can be applied to meet the challenge. Ours is to make the students build and study a scale model of a software project. By scale model, we refer to the kind of object used, for instance, in aerodynamics: small, undetailed, upon which experiments can be conducted and whose relations with the real object are based on similarities rather than straight scale ratio. It must be noted that the students themselves are part of the scale model in our domain.

The concept of the software project as a scale model has several advantages. First, the rules of the game are clearly stated: the students must not produce a program at all cost, but must produce a working team. Next, the self-observation of the project during its life allows experiments to be performed: for instance, to modify some constraints or to try a new organization scheme. Lastly, the students, inevitably confronted with problems in the project, are very receptive to the lectures presenting tools regarding their problem. Also, they are able to put these tools into practice very quickly and to judge their real worth.

4 An experiment: the teamwork project

Since the beginning of the "DESS en Génie Logiciel", a teamwork project has been integrated in the curriculum. This project has greatly evolved during the last four years. Initially, we have upgraded classical academic projects without modifying their spirit. We have also experimented with different schemes of organization such as competing teams or the whole class being one team managed by a member of the teaching staff. As a whole, we have noted that despite the fact that we get satisfactorily technical results, we failed in part to evoke a professional attitude.

The new design of the teamwork project started with the noting that we cannot provide the students with a realistic professional environment: client-producer relations, salary pressure, economic measures, projects spanning several years, existing hierarchies, and so on, are absolutely out of our reach. Rather than building a simulation of such an environment, we preferred the following scale model analogy. The principal difference between the two approaches is that, in the first instance, the students must find a behavior compatible with the rigid frame which is in place, while in the second, they are given the set of parameters which define the project frame, and which the students can experiment with.

Rather than presenting the chronology of the project, we will try to discuss the parameters and explain their actual "value".

4.1 Fixed parameters

The first parameter is the relation between the teaching staff and the students. The staff is composed of four people: three academic teachers and a professional who gives the project management lectures. Two of us play the role of direction managers: they follow the progress of the project, they judge the work, and they can take decisions about the whole project such as allowing a delay or redefining the goals. Naturally, they refuse to take project management decisions. A formal meeting, involving only the project manager and the project administrator, is scheduled on a weekly basis. The third of us is the technical consultant whose role is to help the students when confronted with a technical problem and to judge the quality of the results. The fourth is the management consultant whose role is to help the students structure and analyze the project. The most innovative point in this framework is the hierarchical communication channel which is imposed. Its aim is to produce and make sensible upstream and downstream flows of information, and then to initiate communication structuring.

The second parameter is the theme of the project. This year, it is the implementation of a preprocessor and a programming environment for an object oriented language similar to Objective-C[2]. The theme was chosen because it does not require new technical knowledge from the students: they have all followed a compiler construction course, the tools of the environments can be derived from existing and known tools. The object-oriented flavour of the language is the grain of salt which, because it is fashionable, helps the students find the theme new and interesting. The main advantage of such a theme lies in the fact that the students are able to reuse their previous experience to estimate the size of the modules, to get a first idea of their interaction and to measure the progress of the work.

The third parameter is the set of documents we ask them to produce as a result: informal requirements, general design, detailed design, user's documentation (with an introduction to object oriented programming), usual technical documentation, quality evaluation reports, cost evaluation (time spent) and team progress reports. The last three reports are a novelty to students. Their role is to force the students to analyze the running project. They have also induced an unforseen side-effect: collecting the data to build the reports necessitates a kind of organization which is rejected as bureaucratic. The team manager has then to find a way to get this organization accepted without imposing it. This exemplifies the kind of inter-personal problems which appear in a working team, and their psychology-based solution.

The last parameter concerns the software tools. We imposed the use of MacProject on the project manager and the programming environment ATELIX[3] for the software development. We chose these tools because of their real professional use. At one time, we thought of imposing other tools such as LaTeX [Lam86]for the preparation and editing of written documents or MENTOR [DGHKL80], a syntax directed editor, for the writing of programs, but the necessary learning time would have been too high.

---

[2]Objective-C is a trademark of Stepstone Corporation

[3]ATELIX is the in-house programming environment developed by TELIC-ALCATEL, a French manufacturer of major telephonic equipment

4.2   Flexible parameters

In essence, the value of the flexible parameters can be changed during the teamwork project. This is the strength of the scale model approach, but it could also become a weakness: were the values changed haphazardly or in an incoherent manner, the project would collapse and ruin the pedagogic goals. Thus, these parameters can only be changed by the teaching staff to a value proposed by the students. Naturally, a change must be justified and argued by the team. Two advantages follow from this protocol: we keep the project under control and the students must really understand what is going on in the project. In practice, since the students do not have sufficient experience to criticize their work fully, we give constant feedback on their work during the weekly meetings and by commenting upon all the draft versions of their documents in order to initialize their thinking. Let us now see the different parameters.

A very important parameter is the structure of the team. The previous years showed that we cannot let the students organize themselves and that we cannot freeze a team structure once and for all. Therefore, we imposed a structure at the beginning of the project: a project manager, a project administrator (in charge of ATELIX), a quality group (2), a documentation group (3), a preprocessor group(3) and an environment group(3). Distributing the different tasks and defining the activity of each group were up to the team. The students were allowed to alter this structure only with very strong evidence about its inadequacy, i.e. they must really work within the structure before criticizing it. This setting proved its worth beyond our initial hopes. When it became clear to the team that they could not deliver the project in time, they engaged in negotiation with us to get delays; one of their best arguments was a sound restructuring of the team which reinforced the programming workforce on the preprocessor without sacrificing the rest of the project. Compare this with the too common attitude where everyone rushes on the programming tasks at the end of the assignment.

The second parameter in importance is the size of the software. In a professional context, the size of the software is computed from the client's requirements; the size of the team and the duration of the project are deduced from this estimated size. Since, in our context, the duration and the team are predefined, we choose to work the other way round. It is up to the team to define what they will be able to produce (naturally, we must agree on the proposition!); so, their first task is to write the requirements specification. In the two contexts, the decisive capacity is the same: estimating the size of the final software from its specification. The teamwork project is then a good model of reality with respect to this point. Our aim was to let the students underestimate the software size at the beginning, which they did, and then to resize the software during the expected negotiation on delays. Of course, they had to justify the resizing by precise estimations.

The third parameter is the content of the documents which are required. The organization of the documents is left for the team to decide. They are not required to use plan stereotypes. They can organize the document production as they will. Our task is mostly to stress the inconsistencies within and between the documents, and to ask for better versions. This approach presents several advantages. If a particular document is not completed, this does not block the whole project: for instance, the general design of the processor can be reworked even when the environment group has passed this point. It gives the students sufficient time to understand the aim of each document. It permits us to keep the same team structure during the entire life of the project.

The fourth parameter is time. It has two components: the scheduling of the tasks and deadlines. These two components are left free to the students. The use of project management tools (MacProject and activity reports) allows them to control the project progress and to justify their organization of the time. The evolution of this parameter is mostly made by successive refinements. At the beginning of the project, we require the drawing of a provisional, undetailed, PERT graph. Then, this graph must be completed with the actual data on the past side, and refined for the future side. Thus the students have a precise view of the project at all times; this proves very stimulating. The timetable of deadlines is determined by the students; we allow some alterations, which must be justified. This implies that the team exploits the PERT graph and the activity reports, and does not consider them as "profs' fancy requirements".

The fifth parameter is the structure of the tasks. This parameter also has two components: the determination of the tasks and their partitioning. As it is the case with time, the tools allow the student fine control over these parameters. With the partitioning problem, they discovered one of the uses of the activity reports: to maintain a uniform workload among the participants of the team.

The last parameter is the team communication. As for the fourth and fifth parameters, we do not impose any rigid structure, but we ask the team to report about this aspect of the project. At the beginning of the project, we provide them with the logistic facilities: rooms, common lockers, photocopy credit, electronic conference systems, etc. Our work is restricted to suggestions about the standardization of the documents, the organization of meetings, document diffusion, and the organization of archives. We have noted that this supple organization, as opposed to the fixed communication organization imposed the previous years, allows the student to build a coherent communication structure. In fact, they have become very conscious of its necessity.

5   In lieu of conclusion

Drawing definitive conclusions after a one year experiment would be presumptuous. Nevertheless, we must criticize it in order to improve the positive points and to correct the negative points. Then, we try to advance some explanations about this year's project.

5.1   Positive points

Without any doubt, the students and we feel that the present teamwork project is a real improvement over those run in the preceding years.

A difficulty in the pedagogic management of a teamwork project is the motivation of the students. The classical academic means are the grades, the awarding of a degree, and the "authoritarian" power of the teachers. From our point of view, such means are incompatible with the professional attitude we want to promote. Then, we rely on psychological levers. The typical DESS student wants to be considered as an adult, not as a student. So, our discourse can be roughly summed up by: "Act as adults to show us you are". Naturally, we cannot say this directly: more tact is required. We also need to keep constant attention on the project, but without interfering with its internal management. Thus, our role was slightly more difficult than we had expected, but our efforts have been largely rewarded by the actual professional behavior of the students at the end of the project.

An interesting side-effect of the teamwork project is the suppression of the project management lectures. In fact, they were replaced by the management consultations during which the theoretical tools, the practical problems and their solutions have been presented as answers to the students' questions. So, the impact of this course has been greatly increased.

This year's project has shown the students real engineering problems. Its main advantage over the preceding years' was the reality of the demonstration: we did not create the problems in an abstract fashion (by setting up unnecessary constraints for instance) and we did not propose any ideal solutions. It was all their own work, success and failures included. Though we do not pretend that they actually master the problems (how could we teach in three months the capacities which require several years of practice to be effective?), we are convinced that they have a sound view about them. So, we can hope that, in the near future, they will be able to identify the problems in their professional context and to introduce the theoretical solutions we taught them.

Forthcoming years will indicate the real impact of this kind of transfer from university to industry.

5.2   Negative points

The teamwork project lasted three months this year. Due to the shortness of the academic year, the project was run in parallel with other courses. Thus the effective time left for the work specific to the project was not sufficient to produce full, professional quality, software. So, we had to spend a lot of time fighting the temptation to abandon the project.

In most of the courses, an assignment is given to the students. Generally, it consists of the writing of a small program exemplifying an important concept or tool. Several of them were to be done during the teamwork project. Thus the students' workload attained some unbearable peaks. They were seriously tempted to sabotage some assignments. Naturally, we could not permit such an attitude, but we needed to find a solution, which was an almost impossible task.

In fact, both the problems are linked to the overall organization of the curriculum. In designing the teamwork project as a scale model experiment, we underestimated the increase, in terms of time and workload, which this new approach would induce on the students.

5.3   Open points

When we started the project, we intentionally set aside several questions since we needed to validate our pedagogical strategy before tackling them. Here are the questions — still unresolved.

A first question concerns an important parameter of the scale model: the size of the team. The students suggested subcontracting the programming development to undergraduate students. We refused because we were afraid of navigating on such uncharted territory; we could not accept the risk of failure. But the idea seems interesting and we are studying the possible impact of subcontractors on the teamwork project.

A second question concerns the grading of the project. We are responsible for the quality of the students' training to the profession. The grading is the expression of this responsibility. In this matter, we cannot rely only on feelings and subjective judgements. A way to answer this question is to develop a control board for the project. This would include technical indicators, such as the document evaluation, or how the provisional time scale drifted, but also some pedagogic indicators, such as the students' involvement. This task is important, but difficult.

A third question concerns the relation between the teamwork project and the rest of the curriculum. We are tempted to organize the entire curriculum around the teamwork project. The advantages would be a full year of engineering training instead of three months, a sufficient time span to tackle bigger problems, and a better preparation of the students for the theoretical lectures. Nevertheless, the difficulties are still numerous. A first, practical one, concerns the pedagogic staff involved in the project: instead of four, it would amount to twenty; it is not clear that we could manage the situation. A second difficulty, more fundamental, is that a failure of the project would be out of the question. Could we keep a project under control for six months? Could we size the software at the beginning so that six months would be sufficient to produce it? Honestly, we cannot answer. So, we will work by a progressive extension of the teamwork project during the following years.

The last question concerns the theme of the project. The ideal project would be a real project proposed by a firm. Just as for the preceding question, we would simply have to succeed. The difficulties of such an enterprise are of the same kind as the preceding ones, with one additional problem : getting the firm involved in the pedagogic management of the project. Nevertheless, we are ready to meet the challenge. Making this kind of project succeed would prove not only our capacity to teach software engineering, but, actually, to create it ourselves!

5.4 Present evolution

While writing this paper, we are beginning a new academic year and, so, launching a new teamwork project. We have kept the same frame and the same theme, introducing three improvements:

- since the team size is 16 students (3 more than last year), the extra work-force has been put in the pre-processor group. We suggest that this "big" group be organized in three pairs corresponding to the parsing, the code-generation and the run-time. Thus we hope to break the bottleneck we had noted last year.

- the teamwork project will last 4 months (1 more than last year). During this extra month, each student must become the team "expert" in a specific topic and a specific tool related to the project. At the end of this preliminary stage, the team is required to produce the general framework of the project and its internal standards. Thus we hope to have a quicker start of the proper project work.

- we have introduced a more formal frame of team and personal assessment. Whether or not we should include a form of team self assessment (as described in [JB89] for instance) in our frame remains an open question.

Acknowledgements

This work would not have been possible without the contribution of many people to which we wish to address our most grateful thanks. On top of the list is Gérald Masini, our Object Oriented guru, who acts the difficult role of technical consultant. Next are all the people who tried to bring this text to a readable state. After come our colleagues, who have been forced to cope with our project because of careless increase of the student workload. Following is TÉLIC-ALCATEL which has kindly provided us with ATELIX. Last, but not least, are the students whose enthusiasm was a great support.

References

[DGHKL80] V. Donzeau-Gouge, G. Huet, G. Kahn, and B. Lang. Programming environnement based on structure editors: The MENTOR experience. In *Proc. Workshop on Programming Environments*, Ridge Fields, LT, June 1980.

[HW77] J.J. Horning and D.B. Wortman. Software hut: a computer program engineering project in a form of a game. *IEEE — Trans. Soft. Eng*, 3(4):325–330, 1977.

[JB89] A. Jones and M. Birtle. An individual assessment technique for group projects in software engineering. *Software Engineering Journal*, 4(4):225–232, 1989.

[Kin89] P.J.B. King. Experiences with group project in software engineering. *Software Engineering Journal*, 4(4):221–225, 1989.

[Lam86] L. Lamport. LaTeX *User's Guide & Reference Manual*. Addison-Wesley, 1986.

[MB73] H.D. Mills and F.T. Baker. Chief programmer teams. *Datamation*, 19(12):58–61, DECEMBER 1973.

[Tom89] B. Tompsett. The system cottage — a multidisciplinary engineering group practical. *Software Engineering Journal*, 4(4):209–220, 1989.

[WF76] A.I. Wasserman and P. Freeman, editors. *Towards Improving Software Engineering Education*. Springer-Verlag, New-York, 1976.

[Wor87] D.B. Wortman. Software projects in an academic environment. *IEEE — Trans. Soft. Eng*, 13(11):1176–1181, 1987.

An Experience of Teaching Concurrency: looking back, looking forward

David Bustard
Queen's University, Belfast

Abstract

The book *Concurrent Program Structures*, published in 1988 [1], was based on a course, *Concurrent Systems*, introduced at Queen's University, Belfast in 1981. The purpose of this paper is to examine the successful and less successful aspects of that course, with a view to making improvements to the material presented. A revised edition of *Concurrent Program Structures* is planned.

Introduction

In the 1960s and 1970s the topic of 'concurrency' tended to be brought to the attention of undergraduates in courses on operating systems. Even today, this is still often the case but in the intervening years there has been a growing acceptance that the concept of concurrent behaviour in computing systems has a much wider relevance than the limited context in which it has traditionally appeared.

At Queen's University, Belfast, a final year *Concurrent Systems* course was introduced in 1981 as a direct replacement for a course on operating systems. The material developed for the *Concurrent Systems* course formed the basis of the undergraduate textbook *Concurrent Program Structures*, which appeared in 1988 [1]. The main purpose of this paper is to reflect on the strengths and weaknesses of the course in preparation for a revised edition of the book. The first section of the paper summarises the structure of the course, its objectives and its key features. The second section highlights those aspects of the course that appear to have been most successful. The final section identifies areas which have been in some way unsatisfactory and discusses possible improvements.

Concurrent Program Structures is aimed at second year students - the level at which the course is currently given. The person now responsible for the course has made some modifications to its content and structure but a radical revision of the undergraduate programme is in progress and more changes are expected. This paper covers the major changes that are being considered.

Course Summary

The course, described in *Concurrent Program Structures*, starts by discussing the various forms of concurrency that can occur ranging from that visible to the system designer down to parallelism in the implementation of individual machine instructions. One of the main messages delivered at this stage is that *concurrency is normal* - meaning that concurrent behaviour can be found in all systems, at some level of their operation. Indeed, strictly speaking, there is really no such thing as a sequential system!

A distinction is drawn between systems that are *inherently concurrent*, in that they reflect or respond to real-world activities that occur unpredictably, and those whose concurrency is designed to take advantage of hardware that supports parallel processing. Following this distinction, the course then concentrates exclusively on the inherently concurrent case, covering real-time/embedded systems, operating systems and process-oriented discrete event simulation. These specific application areas are addressed in the second half of the course after a treatment of the general principles and techniques that are common to their construction.

The execution of concurrent systems is discussed as the problem of mapping software processes to hardware processors in different circumstances. Multiprocessors with shared and local memory are considered, as are single processor machines in which concurrency is simulated by switching the processor regularly from one process to another.

The design of concurrent systems is treated using a modular, hierarchical, object-oriented approach, that identifies interacting areas of responsibility in a system [2]. This approach is largely independent of the implementation language chosen and can be used for the development of either concurrent or sequential systems.

The course then considers how such modular designs might be represented in a programming notation. A discussion of the representation of concurrent behaviour is very often introduced by presenting a history of the development of notations, ranging from earliest times to modern day. In the *Concurrent Systems* course, however, the approach taken was to present a specific modern notation and cover the historical perspective at a later stage. The main argument in favour of this latter approach is that students are usually in a better position to compare and evaluate notations once they have some practical experience with at least one of them. The notation presented is Pascal Plus [3], a monitor-based language, similar to Concurrent Euclid [4] and Concurrent Pascal [5]. Pascal Plus was designed and implemented in the late 1970s and it is still used today as much as ever. Its continued use is, however, beginning to pose some problems and a discussion of this point is pursued at length in a later section.

On completing a consideration of the representation of concurrent behaviour, the course then tackles the concepts and techniques associated with the management of process interaction. Two classes of interaction are identified:

- *direct interaction*, where processes actively attempt to make contact with each other, using either synchronised or buffered communication techniques; and
- *indirect interaction*, where processes compete for access to shared resources. A number of different resource management situations are considered, covering the administration of static, dynamic and virtual resources. In each case the central problems of avoiding *starvation* and handling *deadlock* are explored.

After covering the general techniques for designing and implementing concurrent systems, attention is focused on the specific application areas of *discrete event simulation*, *real-time/embedded systems* and *operating systems*, in that order. The distinguishing characteristics of each application area are presented and illustrated appropriately.

The course concludes with a review of the different approaches to the representation of process interaction. The topics covered include *semaphores*, *conditional critical regions*, *monitors* and *rendezvous* mechanisms. In practice, this final topic is largely an evaluation of the concurrency features of Ada [see e.g. 6]

When given as a final year course, additional material dealing with traditional aspects of operating systems was covered. For example, two of the topics discussed are memory management and an examination of the structure and operation of the runtime nucleus (kernal) of an operating system. Note, however, that none of this material has been included in the *Concurrent Program Structures* textbook [1].

Four exercises were set during the course. Most of these appear as exercises in [1] but some are used as illustrative examples in the main text. The first exercise each year required students to produce a design for one or more concurrent systems. The remaining three exercises involved the development of a concurrent program highlighting some central concurrency concept. These latter exercises proved to be very popular because they generally dealt with the modelling of real-world situations with which the students could readily identify. One particularly successful exercise, set in the first year of the course, was the construction of a program to simulate the behaviour of an intoxicated porter delivering Christmas cards in a Computer Science Department. Those who are interested in this intriguing problem can find a description of it in Appendix 1 and a solution in [1].

The Good Bits

This section and the one that follows examine, respectively, those aspects of the *Concurrent Systems* course that have proved effective and those where further thought seems desirable. The successful aspects of the course are presented in six sub-sections covering the course concept, its specialisation in inherently concurrent systems, its classification of process interaction, its approach to presenting language detail, its use of illustrative case studies and the technique for explaining concurrent interaction problems through playacting.

Course Concept

The basic concept of a course dedicated to a treatment of concurrency has worked well. The topic is relevant to all application areas and can be treated generally without setting it in the context of any particular field. Indeed, once treated generally, it is possible to have a greater appreciation of what exactly distinguishes one specific application area from another.

Course Specialisation

The separation of concurrent systems into *inherently concurrent* and *machine-oriented* types has proved to be very clean, allowing each class of system to be considered independently. A course covering machine-oriented concurrency could be given before, after or in parallel with the type of course described in this paper.

Process interaction classification

The separation of process interaction into *direct* and *indirect* types, and their further classification into a small number of distinct cases, has enabled the subject matter to be covered in a systematic and coherent manner. The following table, for example, shows how resource management has been handled:

	Single Resource Required	Multiple Resources Required
a.	One resource defined	---
b.	One resource from N identical resources	M resources from N identical resources
c.	One resource from a subset of N similar resources	M resources from a subset of N similar resources
d.	---	M resources from sets of different resource

The table identifies four types of resource requirement situation (*a.* to *d.*), separating the case where only one resource of a particular type is needed at a time from that were multiple resources of the same or different types are required simultaneously. A Pascal Plus monitor was developed for each case identified, using the following general template:

```
monitor ResourceControl;
  { assumes const PriorityLimit = limit on priority range }

  type *PriorityRange = 0..PriorityLimit;

  procedure *PriorityTryToAcquire (P: PriorityRange; var OK: Boolean ...);
    { Try to obtain resources, using the specified priority P, returning an indication of the
      success, or otherwise, of the operation in OK.}
```

```
procedure *TryToAcquire (var OK: Boolean ...);
    { Try to obtain resources, using the default priority, "PriorityLimit div 2", returning an
      indication of the success, or otherwise, of the operation in OK.}

procedure *PriorityAcquire (P: PriorityRange ...);
    { Try to obtain resources, using the specified priority P, waiting, if necessary until the
      resources are available. }

procedure *Acquire (...);
    { Try to obtain resources, using the default priority, "PriorityLimit div 2", waiting, if
      necessary until the resources are available. }

procedure *Release (...);
    { Release resources; it is assumed that the resources have been acquired previously by
      the releasing process.}

begin
    { initially, prepare for resource requests }
end {ResourceControl};
```

Monitor operations are provided for the acquisition and release of resources. A process may make a tentative attempt to acquire resources (using *PriorityTryToAcquire* or *TryToAcquire*) or wait until resources are available (using *PriorityAcquire* or *Acquire*). In either case the attempt to obtain resources may be made with a default priority or an explicitly stated priority.

Language presentation

The technique used to present the definition of Pascal Plus, the main illustrative language of the course, worked well. The syntax and basic language semantics were given and illustrated directly, with more advanced semantic issues addressed in a *question and answer* session. Here the students were asked to consider the meaning (effect) of a range of code fragments, each of which was developed to highlight a particular language issue. This approach proved to be substantially more effective than presenting the full language directly, without interaction. The (now) obvious advantage is that through discussion students are given an opportunity to (in effect) participate in language design which for many is considerably more interesting than simply absorbing language detail.

Needlesstosay the *question and answer* technique can be used in many other circumstances since it is neither specific to the course nor to the Pascal Plus language.

Illustrative case studies

The case studies used to introduce the main concepts and techniques covered by the course have been developed and refined over a number of years to a point where the subject matter can be conveyed in a simple and effective manner. For example the following range of topics and points are covered with the aid of only two case studies:

a. showing the relationship between design and representation for a monitor-based language;
b. illustrating all of the main features of Pascal Plus; and
c. illustrating that, in concurrent systems, it is preferable for a process to attempt an operation on shared data and fail, rather than inspect the data in order to decide whether the operation should be performed. (The problem is that the data may change between its inspection and the instigation of the subsequent dependent operation.)

The two case studies are:
1. a *temperature/humidity monitoring* system, which measures and displays both the temperature and humidity in a room and sounds an alarm bell if either value exceed some defined bounds; and
2. a *car park control* system, which controls entry to and exit from a car park.

Dijkstra's classic *dining philosophers'* problem (Appendix 2) is used when discussing ways of avoiding deadlock. However, this is not the main motivating example because the students tend to be distracted by peculiarities of the situation. Questions asked include: Why do the philosophers need two forks to eat the spaghetti? Why not avoid deadlock by buying a plentiful supply of forks? Why not alleviate the situation by allowing the forks to be moved around the table? Are the philosophers re-using the forks without cleaning them! ... and so it goes on. The following alternative examples, developed for the course, have proved to be less distracting but equally entertaining:

Toolbox problem

A group of workmen share a single toolbox. When a workman is given a job to do he goes to the toolbox and selects the tools he needs. If any are missing he waits until they have been returned. One day two workmen approach the toolbox together, both needing a hammer and a chisel. Both are ill-mannered and unfriendly. Being ill-mannered they rummage through the toolbox at the same time, with one picking up the hammer and the other the chisel. Being unfriendly, they make no attempt to talk to each other while waiting for the appearance of the tool they lack, and so fail to appreciate that they have the same needs. At the end of the day the supervisor finds them standing idly by the toolbox and, being unfamiliar with the subtleties of resource management problems, fires them.

Wedlock Problem

Two couples, whom we will refer to by the letters A and B (for the sake of anonymity), decide, independently, to get married on the same day in the same church and use the same hotel for their reception after the ceremony. Couple A book the church first while couple B start by booking the hotel. Couple A succeed in booking the church but then find that the hotel is not available because couple B have booked it. To recover, couple A reserve the hotel for the following day with the intention of returning to the church to adjust their booking there accordingly. Meanwhile, couple B, who have booked the hotel first, find that the church is not free on that day and so advance their church booking to the following day, hoping also to move the hotel booking forward one day. The situation is now equivalent to the initial position. If this strategy is continued it will lead to a 'wedlock deadlock' in which neither couple will succeed in marrying unless one pair give up in disgust or decide that they are becoming too old to make the step worthwhile.

Neither problem can claim to be a realistic concern but at least it is possible to believe that such situations *could* occur.

Large Scale Animation
The most successful teaching technique developed for the course was the simulation of complex process interactions using student 'volunteers' to represent processes. An area of the lecture theatre was marked out as a monitor (typically) and the students were required to perform actions on the monitor consistent with its purpose and basic definition (only one active process present at any time). Through such a large-scale animation students were able to get inside concurrent systems (literally!) and so obtain a good appreciation of the interaction problems involved. The entertainment value of the animations was also an important motivating factor - one that relied to some extent on the careful selection of 'processes'. In 1985, for example, the class conveniently provided identical twins (Ann and Maura McPartlan) who were able to serve as two instances of the same process.

Opportunities for Improvement

From the discussion in the preceding section it might be assumed that the current section would be relatively short! Satisfaction is expressed with the concept of a course dedicated to concurrency, with the decision to specialise in inherently concurrent systems, with the systematic approach to the treatment of inter-process communication and resource management, with the suitability of the case studies used and with the manner of presenting language details. Only one problem was touched on, that of the choice of illustrative programming language for the course. This is actually the major problem, with the only other substantial area of concern being the absence of formality in the specification and design of concurrent systems. Each of these topics is now considered in turn.

Major Illustrative Language
It is perhaps ironic that when the *Concurrent Systems* course was first introduced, its use of Pascal Plus could be regarded as one of its strengths. The language was developed locally to meet the needs of a number of courses and subsequently evolved to match changes in those needs [15]. The language is thus 'ideal' for the *Concurrent Systems* course in that the two are well matched. The language is still useful for that reason, but it has not been possible to keep pace with advances in technology and methodology that have occurred. Specifically,

the following problems have been experienced:

1. *Pascal Plus is not adequately supported*

   As has been stated, Pascal Plus is a local development, which means that local resources are needed to keep the language and its implementations up to an adequate standard. This means introducing or refining language features as necessary and also ensuring that adequate language specific tools are available to support program development. In practice, most effort has gone into porting the compiler and other tools from one machine to another. This task has become tedious and also increasingly more expensive because of the ever-expanding size of the system involved. The expansion, however, has not been sufficient to keep pace with the demands of modern software development methods which require sophisticated tools, with sophisticated interfaces. It has proved impossible to meet these demands on a typical university development budget.

2. *Pascal Plus has serious competitors*

   When Pascal Plus was first developed, all languages with direct support for concurrency were essentially 'experimental' and Pascal Plus could legitimately claim to be as good as any of its competitors. Now, however, there are several languages, such as Ada and Modula-2 [7], that have better support (available commercially, at reasonable cost and running on commonplace hardware), leaving Pascal Plus as the language choice only of those who find its technical features particularly attractive. Without adequate support, however, even these enthusiasts will wane.

3. *Pascal Plus is not widely used*

   Students are required to have a good grasp of Pascal Plus in order to complete the practical exercises that are set. Many would prefer to put this effort into a language that they might encounter later in their careers.

4. *Pascal Plus supports a limited view of concurrent system design*

   Pascal Plus enables concurrent systems to be constructed as a set of processes that interact indirectly through monitors. All systems *can* be constructed this way but for some applications indirect communication is a distortion of the system design. Thus, it would be desirable to provide facilities that support direct communication when required. Pressure to have such facilities has increased steadily as the direct communication style of representation has progressively gained more followers.

All of the factors outlined above continue to grow in importance so it seems certain that Pascal Plus will have to be replaced or, at least, its key role diminished. Ada is perhaps the most obvious contender as a replacement language. Certainly it avoids the first three criticisms levelled at Pascal Plus by being well supported, ahead of most of its competitors and widely used. However, like Pascal Plus, it supports only one approach to concurrent system design - that of direct process communication. It is also a higher level language than Pascal Plus which makes certain activities, such as the priority allocation of resources, difficult to represent elegantly. Should a change from Pascal Plus to Ada be made it would probably be necessary to change the current order of presentation of some material and, in particular, discuss techniques for dealing with process communication before resource management. It might also be desirable to discuss a monitor-based language before starting the latter topic. Pascal Plus might be introduced at this point or perhaps Modula-2 [7] used with concurrency features simulated following the Pascal Plus process/monitor model. This latter option is perhaps more attractive because Modula-2 is now the introductory undergraduate programming language at Belfast.

Introduction of Formality

The Concurrent Systems course was designed for second year students who often have little knowledge of a formal, mathematical approach to software development. The trend in undergraduate courses, however, is towards greater formality at all levels and in all courses. To keep pace with this trend it seems essential to introduce a formal approach to the specification, design and verification of concurrent software. A full formal treatment of concurrency is likely to occupy a course by itself [e.g see 8, 9] so only the basic concepts and notations involved could be covered in the time available.

To avoid extending the course unduly it would be desirable to use a sympathetic formal notation/programming language pair such that a coverage of the formal notation would also serve to introduce the main concepts of the programming language. Since all of the major formal specification notations, CSP [8], CCS [9] and LOTOS [11] are based on a directly communicating process model, Ada once again emerges as a suitable choice of introductory programming language. Another possibility is occam [10] which is very closely modelled on CSP [8]. The availability of occam is currently quite limited and so it is perhaps not a serious contender as the main programming language but it is still worthy of discussion because of its special role in programming transputers.

Many features of CSP, CCS or LOTOS can be translated mechanically into Ada or occam, thereby enabling a relatively smooth transition from specification/design into coding. A discussion of this topic may be found in [12] which considers, in particular, the translation of designs expressed in LOTOS into Ada.

Another suggestion for increased formality is in the diagrammatic representation of concurrent systems. At the highest level of description it would probably be useful to discuss system behaviour in terms of Petri nets [13]. These tend to become unwieldy for large systems but work well for the type of small educational examples that are often quoted. Again, only an introduction to Petri nets could be covered in the time available.

One problem with introducing formal methods into an undergraduate course is the current lack of tool support for the notations involved. The facilities needed are the sort usually provided for any programming language, such as an editor, syntax and semantic checker. An animation facility for examining the meaning of a formal specification [14] is also desirable.

Much of what appears in this section relates to notational issues. This is perhaps not surprising because notations are needed to express and discuss system specifications, designs and coding, which accounts for a substantial part of any concurrent systems course. Notations are recognised, however, as a constant source of danger to the educator in that without meticulous planning it is possible to construct a course around a single language, as has tended to happen with Pascal Plus in the *Concurrent Systems* course. However, the problem is not necessarily alleviated by using a range of languages because then a course can degenerate into a comparative language study. The responsibility is left with the course designer to ensure that all the required general principles and techniques are covered in a language independent manner and then later stressed when illustrated in the notations that are used.

Conclusion

This paper has evaluated a long-standing course on concurrency, identifying those aspects of the course that appear to have been successful and two major aspects of the course where change seems necessary: the addition of greater formality and the use of a different illustrative programming language. These two changes are related in that the programming and formal notations selected should be reasonably sympathetic. For this reason Ada is a good choice for the programming language because it fits together well with the major formal notations. The choice of formal notation is still an open question but LOTOS [11] is a strong contender because it has an ISO standard for its definition.

Overall, it is tempting to conclude that the *Concurrent Systems* course has been an outstanding success! The course has been enjoyable to present and the students have found the material interesting, as reflected in their enthusiasm in class and in their efforts to complete the practical and tutorial exercises. The course objectives seem sound and by incorporating the changes suggested in the preceding section the material should become even more relevant to the needs of the software engineers of the future.

Acknowledgements

Thanks are due to John Elder and Jim Welsh, co-authors of *Concurrent Program Structures* and to Professor C.A.R Hoare who provided inspiration both for the textbook and the *Concurrent Systems* course that preceded it. The author is also grateful to Howard Johnston who presented the course several times and who consequently made many useful suggestions for improvement.

References

1 Bustard, D.W., Elder, J.W.G. and Welsh, J.: *Concurrent Program Structures*, Prentice Hall International, 1988

2 Parnas, D.L., *On the criteria to be used in decomposing systems into modules*, CACM, Vol. 15, pp 1053-1058, 1972; reprinted in Freeman, P. and Wasermann, A.I., *Tutorial on Software Design Techniques*, 4th edn., IEEE, 1983

3 Welsh, J. and Bustard, D.W., *Pascal Plus: another language for modular multiprogramming*, Software Practice and Experience, Vol. 9, pp 947-957, 1979

4 Holt, R.C., *Concurrent Euclid, the UNIX system and TUNIS*, Addison Wesley, 1983

5 Brinch Hansen, P., The Architecture of Concurrent Programs, Prentice Hall, 1977

6 Watt, D.A., Wichmann, B.A. and Findlay, W., Ada Language and Methodology, Prentice Hall, 1987

7 Wirth N, *Programming in Modula-2* (3rd edn), Springer Verlag, Berlin, 1985

8 Hoare, C.A.R.: *Communicating Sequential Processes*, Prentice Hall International, 1985

9 Milner, R.: Communication and Concurrency, Prentice Hall International, 1989

10 Inmos Ltd, *occam Programming Manual*, Prentice Hall International, 1984

11 Brinksma, E. (Ed.): *Information processing systems - Open systems interconnection - LOTOS - A Formal Technique Based on the Temporal Ordering of Observational Behaviour*, ISO DIS 8807, Jul. 1987

12 Bustard D.W., Norris M.T. & Orr R.A.,: *Formalising the Design of Ada Systems using LOTOS*, Proceedings of the 1989 Ada Europe Conference, Madrid, June 1989

13 Reisig, W., *Petri Nets: an introduction*, Springer-Verlag, 1982

14 Patel S., Orr R.A., Norris M.T. & Bustard D.W.,: *Tools to Support Formal Methods*, in Proceedings of the Eleventh International Conference on Software Engineering, May 1989

15 Bustard, D.W.: *Pascal Plus in Biased Perspective*, in proceeding of the IFIP Working Conference on *System Implementation Languages: Experience and Assessment*, (North Holland, 1985)

Appendix 1: The Drunken Porter Problem

On the first day of December each year the eight teaching staff (of a typical Computer Science Department) prepare Christmas cards to send to each other. The cards are posted at a central mail-box from where they are collected and distributed by a porter. Unfortunately the porter always starts celebrating early and makes some mistakes during each delivery. Specifically, instead of delivering the cards according to the office numbers on the envelopes he unloads a bundle of cards at random in each office. On reaching the final office he 'completes' his delivery by leaving all the cards that remain.

The offices are laid out in a rectangle with a surrounding corridor as shown in the following diagram.

The porter always follows the corridor in a clockwise direction starting his delivery at office number 1.

Some cards by chance reach their correct destination but most are returned to the central mail-box for redistribution. All returns are made before the porter's next delivery.

If the state of the porter does not improve is it likely that all the cards will be delivered by Christmas, assuming that he makes four deliveries per day for 18 working days?

Is the result different if he staggers at the junction in the corridor so that some deliveries are made in an anticlockwise direction?

Construct a simulation model to help answer these questions.

Appendix 2: The Dining Philosophers Problem

The Dining Philosophers problem (posed by E.W.Dijkstra) is one of the standard examples used to illustrate how deadlock and starvation can occur (and be avoided) in concurrent programs. The problem is usually specified in terms of five philosophers who spend their time either eating or thinking. They eat at a single communal table where each has a reserved place. The table is laid out thus:

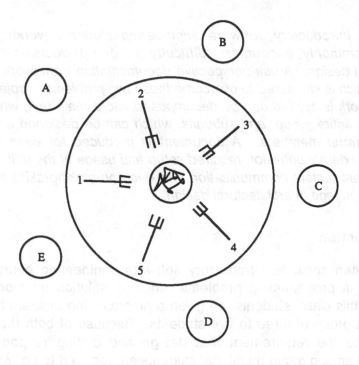

Spaghetti is the only type of food provided and it is so knotted that two forks are needed to eat it. In all, five forks are available but each philosopher is only permitted to pick up the fork on either side of his or her seat. Thus, for example, philosopher A must eat with forks 1 and 2.

The problem is to devise a way of using the forks so that deadlock and starvation are prevented. In this problem the starvation is literal. If the philosophers can pick up forks one at a time there is a danger, for example, that all five philosophers will attempt to pick up their left forks simultaneously, causing deadlock, and so starve to death waiting for their right forks to appear. Alternatively, if a philosopher is permitted only to pick up the forks when both are available then starvation is still possible if his or her neighbours eat alternately without interruption, since the two forks required are never available simultaneously.

Use-Perspective Unit Documentation

Frank A. Cioch   Fatma Mili

Department of Computer Science and Engineering
Oakland University
Rochester, MI 48309
email: CiochFA@unix.secs.oakland.edu

Abstract. *Introductory software engineering students working on larger projects commonly encounter difficulty in group decision-making and architectural design. A use-perspective documentation framework is taught to students which is structured to overcome these two problems. Projects to which this framework is applied can be decomposed into a main unit, which requires input of the entire group, and subunits, which can be designed and coded by individual group members. A document is produced for each of the units concerning external behavior, required setup and usage of the unit. Creation of this document fosters communication and decision-making skills and requires students to engage in architectural design.*

1. Introduction

Students often come to introductory software engineering courses with no experience in programming problems requiring solution by more than one person. In this class, students are given a programming problem that must be solved by a group of three to five students. Because of both the size of the problem and the requirement that design and coding responsibilities be apportioned among group members, students are required to do two things that are new to them: 1) they must communicate with each other during the design process; and 2) they must perform architectural design in order to decompose the program into units that can be developed by individual students.

Experience teaching the class has shown that there are two difficulties that are commonly encountered and need to be explicitly addressed during the class: 1) Because of students' lack of experience in working with others, groups have difficulty making decisions. Either a group tries to make every single decision together or a "super-programmer" type of student takes over the design and coding responsibilities and makes all of the decisions alone; and 2) Because their experience is limited to small programming problems, students tend to skip architectural design and proceed directly to algorithm development. Design documentation is often produced after coding rather than during design.

In an effort to address these issues, a documentation framework is taught to the students along with architectural design techniques. The framework is a modification of a documentation framework that has been developed and used for systems integration [1], reuse [2] and decision support [3].

The framework is used to document software units during the design and implementation phases of the life cycle. The documentation serves as a communication tool during design. Students are instructed to develop user documentation for the designers/programmers who develop, debug, or modify units that must interact with the unit being documented. By requiring students to write user documentation, they can build on experiences they have had with end-user documentation.

The content of the documentation is at the architectural design level, as it contains information concerning the interaction between the unit and its environment. Three features of software units that are relevant to their interaction with the environment are used to structure the documentation: what the unit does (output considerations), how to use the unit (input considerations), when to use the unit. The reasons underlying every aspect of the unit's interaction with the environment are also provided.

Section 2 of the paper contains a description of the course in which the documentation framework is used. In Sections 3 and 4 the documentation framework is described and an example is provided. Finally, in Section 5, the value of the documentation to the students is discussed.

2. Course Description

The course in which this documentation framework is being used is Introduction to Software Engineering. It is attended by both senior-level undergraduate students and graduate students at Oakland University. The course is taught from a practitioner's perspective with a term project as the focal point. Students work on the project in groups of three to five students per group. Both Fairley [4] and Pressman [5] have been used as textbooks.

At the beginning of the course the instructor gives the students a short verbal description of a product that needs to be defined and developed. During the first half of the term the instructor plays the role of client and uses one third to one half the lecture time interacting with the groups in this role. Each group is responsible for interacting with the client, learning what the client's needs are, and defining the product. From these discussions a Requirements Specification document is developed.

The second half of the term is spent developing the product. Each group designs the product from its own Requirements Specification. During this portion of the course the instructor plays the role of technical manager of the project and uses one third to one half the lecture time interacting with the groups in this role. Each group is responsible for producing the documentation and using it to keep the project manager informed during the design phase.

The project is chosen so that it can be decomposed into three to five major units. In this way, the groups are encouraged to break down design and coding responsibilities into a main unit and interacting subunits, where each group member is responsible for a subunit and the group as a whole is responsible for the main unit.

For each unit, a Use-Perspective Unit Document is produced by the student responsible for that unit. The documentation is used as a tool to both resolve architectural design issues and to keep the project manager informed of progress. By requiring that meetings with the project manager be scheduled throughout design, students are required to produce the documentation as the units are being designed.

3. The Use-Perspective Unit Document

The users of a use-perspective document for a unit are designers/programmers of units which will interact with the given unit. The use-perspective for a unit means that the documentation for the unit is written specifically for these users. All aspects of the unit's interaction with the other units (collectively referred to as the environment) are included in the documentation.

Three features of software units that are relevant to their interaction with the environment are used to structure the documentation: 1) what the unit does (behavior or output considerations), 2) how to use the unit (setup or input considerations), and 3) when to use the unit. The rationale underlying every aspect of the unit's interaction with the environment is also provided. The complete structure of the Use-Perspective Unit Document is:

Use-Perspective Unit Document

A. External Behavior
 1. Function; Rationale
 2. Environmental Effects; Rationale
 3. Performance Attributes; Rationale

    B. Required Setup
       1. Use Syntax; Rationale
       2. Preconditions; Rationale
    C. Usage; Rationale

External Behavior.   The purpose of this section is to list all of the externally observable effects of using the unit. This includes everything that the unit does which impacts the environment. The external behavior of the unit is documented in three subsections: Function, Environmental Effects, and Performance Attributes. The Function subsection is simply a short verbal statement of the functionality provided by the unit. It describes, from the user's point of view, the primary duty or role required of the unit.

The Environmental Effects subsection describes every effect using the unit has on the environment. All externally observable behaviors of the unit are listed in this subsection. For example, a unit whose purpose is to compute the power of a number may also have the effect of preserving the value of the original number. Often, these behaviors are a result of decisions made by the designer of the unit during the design and implementation of the unit. Because these decisions have a potential effect on the environment, the users must be informed of them.

The external behavior of a unit includes not only its actions resulting from its performance, but also characteristics of the performance itself, such as how long it takes to perform its activities. The value of using attribute requirements during software development is described by Gilb [6]. The Performance Attributes subsection lists performance characteristics of the unit. For example, a unit which is intended to compute the power of a number n may run in O(log n) time. Because this performance characteristic has a potential effect on the performance characteristics of units which use this unit, the user should be informed of it.

The reason for each of the behavioral characteristics listed in the External Behavior section are also provided in the documentation. This results in a Rationale section for each of the three subsections. Some behavior characteristics are a result of design decisions made during internal design or implementation of the unit. The designer of the unit should explain why the decision was made. If the decision is arbitrary, this should be mentioned. Other behavior characteristics are a result of decisions made in cooperation with designers of other units. For example, a unit may run in O(log n) time because the users of the unit require the speed.

Required Setup.   The purpose of this section is to provide all of the information about how to use the unit. This includes anything that must be done before the unit will function properly. The setup required of the user is documented in two subsections: Use Syntax and Preconditions. The Use Syntax subsection is directed toward programming considerations and focuses on the syntax of use. The type and purpose of each of the parameters are explained. The names of required files are given along with how the unit is made operational. This subsection may be thought of as a user's manual for the unit.

The Preconditions subsection lists all conditions that must be satisfied before the unit will function properly. For example, a unit which is intended to compute the power of a number may require $O(\log n)$ storage at run time. Some of the preconditions are required to produce the desired function and environmental effects while others are required so that the desired performance attributes are produced. For each precondition, the rationale underlying the precondition is also given. For example, $O(\log n)$ storage is required to produce $O(\log n)$ speed.

Usage. The Usage section is helpful when a user has alternative units to choose from and is trying to decide which one to use. After reading the External Behavior and Required Setup sections the user knows how to use the unit but may still not be certain whether or not to use the unit.

The purpose of the Usage section is to provide a description of characteristics of the environment that affect either the optimal or intended use of the unit. Sometimes, these characteristics can be inferred from other sections and are stated in the Usage section more explicitly and typically, more informally as well. For example, a unit which is intended to compute the power of a number n may work well in an environment where large values of n need to be processed but may not be fast enough in an environment in which only small values of n occur. While the clauses in the Preconditions section are imperative (i.e., unit requires $O(\log n)$ run time storage), the clauses in the Usage section are intended to provide concrete imagery of the characteristics of the environment that the unit was designed to operate in.

A second use of the Usage section is to document the intended use of the unit in order to create the same "look and feel" in all portions of a product. In some cases the users of a unit are expected to use the unit under certain circumstances and an alternative unit in different circumstances. For example, a unit dealing with fatal errors may be expected to be used under different circumstances than a unit dealing with warnings. The intended use would be described in the Usage section of the documentation for the units so that there is uniformity in the way in which errors are handled by the system.

4. An Example

In this section we use a small example to illustrate the development of a Use-Perspective Unit Document during design. Assume that a student is assigned the task of designing and implementing a unit to compute the nth power of a number. The starting point in developing the documentation for the unit is for the student to describe the function of the unit, and the rationale underlying the creation of the unit.

> *Function:*
> -- compute the nth power of a number
> *Rationale:*
> -- task that will be performed many times in the system

Often, this is all that is said by the group and the student assigned the task of designing and implementing the unit begins to design a subprogram to perform the required task. When the syntax has been decided upon, it is documented.

> *Use Syntax:*
> Function NthPower(n : INTEGER; x : REAL): REAL;
> NthPower returns x^n.
> *Rationale:*
> -- A function was used rather than a procedure because the subprogram needs only to compute a single value.

At this point the student discusses and evaluates the decisions with the group. The decisions about the syntax of use have led to the identification of environmental effects and preconditions that must be satisfied in order to use the unit properly.

> *Environmental Effects:*
> -- x and n are unchanged
> *Rationale:*
> -- x and n are unchanged because an arithmetic function should not have "side-effects"

> *Preconditions:*
> -- value to be raised must be a real number
> -- power to raise the value to must be an integer
> *Rationale:*
> -- The value to be raised to a power is real because very large numbers will be processed.
> -- Even though we only expect to be using it for positive integers, the function works for all integers n, in anticipation of a possible future need.

In this example, both the Environmental Effects and the Preconditions can be deduced from the Use Syntax section. This would not be the case if there were preconditions other than type conditions, such as the availability of global variables or routines from a library. In addition, the unit may have behaviors other than those identifiable from the procedure header, such as changing the state of the system or changing global variables. As they were identified, all of these interactions with the environment would be listed in the Environmental Effects and Preconditions sections of the documentation.

During discussions with the group it may have become clear to the designer of the unit that large values of n will be input. As a result, a log n algorithm is designed rather than the obvious algorithm of order n. There is overhead in setting up the log n algorithm so the function is slow for small values of n. It also turns out that local storage is required for the log n algorithm.

The designer has identified a characteristic of the environment in which the unit will be used and this characteristic has led to a design decision that impacts both performance characteristics of the unit and preconditions of using the unit.

Performance Attributes:
-- Algorithm is $O(\log n)$.
Rationale:
-- large values of n are expected to be processed most of the time

Preconditions:
-- Algorithm requires $O(\log n)$ local storage at run time.
Rationale:
-- need the storage to reduce the speed from $O(n)$ to $O(\log n)$.

The Performance Attributes and Preconditions subsections contain factual information. The Usage section gives the designers description of the environment in which the unit is most effectively used. The performance attributes and preconditions become the reasons why the environment should have these characteristics.

Usage:
-- Works well for large values of n, but if n is small, a different approach would have faster speed.
-- If run time memory is tight, a different approach may be preferred.
Rationale:
-- The algorithm is $O(\log n)$, but computational overhead is required to set up the algorithm.
-- Algorithm uses $O(\log n)$ local storage, allocated dynamically at run time.

The designer's approach can be evaluated by the group. The unit is evaluated with respect to the environment in which it will be used. The environment should match the conditions described in the Usage section. This evaluation can be done without knowledge of the specifics of the internal operation. Only the impact of internal functioning on the environment needs to be discussed with the group members.

5. Value to the Students

Based upon both observations made during the project manager role and conversations with the students, it is apparent that using the documentation framework can be of value to students in improving decision-making and fostering architectural design.

1. Students use the framework to judge which design decisions need to be discussed with others and which can be decided upon alone.

The development of the documentation helps the groups make decisions by providing a way to identify those decisions that need to be discussed and those that can be made alone. Only a design decision that affects the interaction between different units needs to be discussed. Only those students working on the interacting units need to participate in the decision. All other decisions can be made alone.

2. Students use the framework as an aid in performing architectural design and evaluating the design's quality.

Production of the documentation requires that the students work at the level of programming-in-the-large and forces students to direct their attention toward the identification of units and interactions between units. Because students have to explicitly identify and carefully write down all interactions between units, there is a built-in incentive for unit independence. As design proceeds, students restructure their units so that coupling between units is reduced. The groups spend time deciding in which unit a task should be performed or a data structure should be defined.

References

[1]   Cioch, F.A. and F. Mili, "Software Documentation for Systems Integration: A Triangular Framework," Oakland University Technical Report, TR-CSE-89-10-01.

[2] Cioch, F.A. and F. Mili, "Use-Oriented Documentation for Reusable Components," presented at the First Great Lakes Computer Science Conference, 1989.

[3] Mili, F. and F.A. Cioch, "Documenting Decision Models for Informed and Confident Decisions," Proceedings of the 23rd Hawaii International Conference on System Sciences, IEEE, 1990.

[4] Fairley, R., Software Engineering Concepts, McGraw-Hill, 1985.

[5] Pressman, R.S., Software Engineering: A Practitioner's Approach, 2nd edition, McGraw-Hill, 1987.

[6] Gilb, T., Principles of Software Engineering Management, Addison-Wesley, 1988.

Panel Discussion:
Graduate Programs in Software Engineering

Moderator:

Gary Ford
Software Engineering Institute

Panel Members:

Alfs Berztiss
Computer Science Department
University of Pittsburgh

Daniel R. Bidwell
Computer Information Science Department
Andrews University

Bernice M. Folz
Dean, Department of Quantitative Methods and Computer Science
College of St. Thomas

Norman E. Gibbs
Professor and Director of Software Engineering Education
Carnegie Mellon University

Daniel Olivier
Intermetrics, Inc.

Panelists discussed the motivation for and structure of the master's curriculum in software engineering at their respective universities (at National University in the case of Mr. Olivier). Short descriptions of these programs follow.

A software engineering program based on engineering principles

A. T. Berztiss and W. D. Hurley
Department of Computer Science
University of Pittsburgh, Pittsburgh, PA 15260

In his "silver bullet" paper Frederick Brooks suggested three fruitful approaches to dealing with the essential difficulties of software development. First, spread costs by developing easily adaptable products. Second, let software systems evolve from rudimentary prototypes. Third, produce great designers. Since great designers are hard to come by, prototypes, and the software that evolves from them, will have to be developed by many competent craftsmen rather than a few outstanding artists. The goal of our MS program in software engineering education is to develop such competence.

Our program is based on the adaptation of standard engineering practices to the development of software with special emphasis on prototyping. Although there is the major difference between conventional and software engineering in that engineers in general produce tangible objects, but software engineers produce abstractions, software engineers engage in the same *activities* as other engineers.

Our purpose was to develop a software engineering curriculum that emphasizes general engineering principles. To this end we first identified ten tasks that engineers perform: (1) define specifications for the objects to be constructed; (2) resolve conflicting requirements and adapt ideal specifications to real-life constraints by setting priorities; (3) construct objects from standard components, or modify standard components to suit special circumstances; (4) anticipate change and make allowances for modifications; (5) transfer theory into practice; (6) scale up, either in production or in size; (7) perform tests in order to maintain the quality of products at predetermined measurable levels, with respect to reliability, robustness, efficiency, testability, modifiability and portability, reusability, understandability, and other quality attributes; (8) determine what tools are needed for a given job; (9) apply management techniques to the previous activities; (10) engage in technological adventure when needed.

Since software engineering is concerned with large-scale software development projects, participation in group projects must be a component of education in software engineering. We emphasize information systems because we think them representative of the systems our students will have to develop in their professional lives. Systems that our groups have built include management systems for a supermarket chain, a metropolitan transit system, and a cultural institution.

The Department of Computer Science has already been offering two graduate courses in software engineering for the past three years:

CS231A   *Specification and Design* introduces a number of specification languages, such as Larch, VDM, Z, and SF, and uses them in specification case studies. Emphasis is on prototyping, and the topics covered include software quality attributes, domain modeling, modularization criteria and the handling of scale-up and maintenance problems, the interplay of modularization and reuse throughout software development, validation of specifications and designs, and knowledge-based system techniques for maintaining specification and design information. The course also covers tools for specification and design. In the future there will no longer be a group project associated with this course. Instead, specification languages will be studied in greater depth.

CS231B   *Implementation and Testing* is a general survey of the field, with emphasis on the conversion of software specifications into software products, and the management of the software development process. Topics include transformational development of software, and quantitative approaches to software quality, under the headings of automatic generation of software, construction of highly modular software, and the enhancement of reuse, of verification and validation, and of testing. An important part of this course is the reading and discussion of technical literature.

This year we have instituted a Master of Science Program in Software Engineering. This program is project oriented and provides more focused education than the traditional Master of Science in Computer Science. A total of ten courses is required. The new program consists of courses from three categories: (1) a core of four software engineering courses; (2) advanced support courses; and (3) fundamental computer science courses. Besides CS231A and CS231B described above, the core contains the following two courses:

CS281   *Information Processing Systems* deals with management of data, information, and knowledge. Topics include information system models and the management of multi-media information, information exchange models and the management of communications, and office procedure models and the management of office activities. Visual specification and knowledge-based software engineering methods for information systems design are two of the techniques discussed.

CS209   *Master's Directed Project* is a project course in which, under faculty supervision, a number of students form a software development team, define a suitable project, and demonstrate their ability to apply the theory and techniques learned in other courses to the completion of the project. This course also provides students with an opportunity to gain practical experience in applying management techniques.

The following advanced support courses deal with techniques that have demonstrated potential for improving the software development process, providing it with new tools, and improving the quality of software products of the future. Two of these courses are required:

CS236	*Modeling and Simulation*
CS255	*Principles of Database Systems*
CS261	*Interface Design and Evaluation*
CS272	*Knowledge Representation*

The category of fundamental support courses provides in-depth treatment of the basic theoretical and scientific concepts relevant to software engineering. It is required to take CS211A or CS215A, and two of CS221A, CS251A, CS254A.

CS211A	*Theory of Computation*
CS215A	*Design and Analysis of Algorithms*
CS221A	*Language Design*
CS251A	*Advanced Computer Operating Systems*
CS254A	*Computer Architecture*

Master of Science in Software Engineering

Daniel R. Bidwell
Andrews University

From 1985 to 1987 the Computer Information Science department participated with the Michiana Chapter of the Data Processing Management Association in a Business / Education Forum to discuss the need for computer professionals in local industry. After reviewing the Wang Institute of Graduate Studies' Master of Software Engineering degree, the Master of Science in Software Engineering was started in 1987. Approximately one third of our graduate students are employed by local industry and attend school part time. Several of our Software Engineering graduates have accepted positions teaching in four-year colleges that have or are establishing Computer Information Systems baccalaureate programs.

The Computer Information Science department has always placed a strong emphasis on applications software development. The undergraduate Computer Information Systems degree has a strong component of business courses.

The Master of Science in Software Engineering places a strong emphasis on developing the skills and knowledge for software development. Two major projects are required. The student must interact with end users to discern their needs and develop a software system to meet those needs, as well as appropriate software and user documentation. Some of the projects involve other departments on campus while many involve applications for local businesses. Some of the projects are combined with major projects at the students place of employment.

The Systems Analysis II and Software Engineering II courses each contain a major group project where teams of students must work together to develop a substantial software product. The students can see first hand the necessities of good communication and written specifications.

Program title

Master of Science in Software Engineering

Entrance requirements

A four-year baccalaureate degree that includes the following undergraduate prerequisites or their equivalent.

Introduction to Computer Science
Elementary Data Structures
Computer Organization
FORTRAN or COBOL
Introduction to Systems Software
Calculus
Discrete Math
Statistics

Degree requirements

A minimum of 48 quarter credits; at least 28 credits chosen from 500- and 600-level graduate courses.

Foundation courses

Foundation courses are 400-level senior/graduate courses that may apply to the graduate program if not already taken as an undergraduate. Each course is 4 quarter credits.

Advanced Data Structures
Data Base Systems
Systems Analysis I
Systems Analysis II
Operating Systems I

Core courses

The following graduate-level courses must be included in the student's program of study. Each course is 4 quarter credits.

Computer Architecture
Software Engineering I
Software Engineering II
Programming Project Management

Projects

Two major projects totaling 8 credits are required. Systems Analysis II and Software Engineering II each have an extensive group project component.

Master of Software Design and Development
Bernice M. Folz, Ph.D.
Department of Quantitative Methods and Computer Science
College of St. Thomas
St. Paul, Minnesota 55105-1096

Bernice M. Folz, Ph.D.
Department of Quantitative Methods and Computer Science
College of St. Thomas
St. Paul, Minnesota 55105-1096

The College of St. Thomas conducted a feasibility study in the spring of 1984 as to the expected need in the metropolitan area for engineers and computer scientists. Included in the feasibility study was a statistical analysis of the results from four groups: chief executive officers (excluding 3M, Honeywell, CDC, Sperry and IBM), personnel department staff, engineers, and managers of engineering personnel. Results from these samples indicated an extremely strong consensus that engineers and computer scientists will be in great demand within the next five years. Sample results indicated that the computer scientist need was greater than the electronic/electrical engineering need. Based on the results of this market research and the concern about the need for well-trained software engineers in Minnesota, the College of St. Thomas decided to begin to address these needs by instituting a Master of Software Design and Development (MSDD).

This master's is applied, workplace oriented rather than research oriented. The program is designed for practitioners in the software area who wish to enhance their skills for their current positions or for career advancement. The program enrolls software professionals who work full time during the day and attend classes in the evenings or weekends. To ensure the practical, applied characteristic of the program, the instructors are experienced software professionals. The program seeks to improve the software development environment by providing knowledge, skill and experience that cannot be gained in the workplace.

The curriculum for the master's program reflects industry requirements. A task force of software professionals from several local companies reviewed the initial course content. Advisory committees from industry assist in the development of each course. This master's program seeks to fill the gap between Management Information Systems (MIS) programs and computer science programs with specific courses to improve the quality of developed software. Students integrate classroom learning with the workplace environment by completing a two-semester "real world" software design and development project.

ADMISSIONS REQUIREMENTS

The Master of Software Design and Development is open to those awarded a bachelor's degree from an accredited college or university. The Admissions Committee considers the following:

- . Minimum of two years of full-time programming or software experience;
- . Official transcripts;
- . Major(s) and minor(s);
- . Graduate entrance examination.

DEGREE REQUIREMENTS

Fourteen courses are needed to satisfy the requirements for the MSDD degree. All classes are three semester credits.

REQUIRED COURSES

- . Technical Communications
- . Software Engineering Methodologies
- . DBMS and Design
- . Systems Analysis and Design I
- . Software Productivity Tools
- . Software Project Management
- . Software Quality Control/Quality Assurance
- . Legal Issues in Technology
- . Project (two semesters)

ELECTIVE COURSES (Four required)

- . Distributed Database Management
- . User Interface Management Systems
- . Data Modeling and Information Analysis
- . Operating Systems Design (UNIX and C)
- . Real-Time Systems and Applications
- . Language Structure and Translators
- . Graphics
- . Microprocessor Fundamentals
- . Modeling, Forecasting, Simulation
- . Artificial Intelligence and Knowledge-Based Systems
- . Software Engineering in Factory Automation (Robotics)
- . Systems Analysis and Design II
- . Strategic Information Systems
- . Accounting, Finance and Economics for Technical Managers
- . Design of an Integrated Corporate Information System
- . Design of an Integrated Manufacturing Information System
- . Telecommunications
- . Seminars
  - End User Computing
  - Software Systems Testing and Requirements
  - Capacity Planning

The Carnegie Mellon University
Master of Software Engineering Degree Program

Norman E. Gibbs, Mark A. Ardis, A. Nico Habermann, James E. Tomayko
Carnegie Mellon University

Overview

Carnegie Mellon University (CMU) offers a professional Master of Software Engineering degree (MSE). This program is a joint effort between the School of Computer Science and the Software Engineering Institute (SEI).

The objective of the MSE program is to produce a small number of highly skilled experts in software system development using an educational paradigm based on a master-apprentice relationship. Its main purpose is to focus on software products and the application of principles from computer science and other related disciplines to truly *engineer* superior products.

The program builds on a solid undergraduate program in computer science (or its equivalent), and requires at least two years experience working on sizable software development efforts. Students are expected to have a solid foundation in discrete mathematics and programming-in-the-small. We require competence in programming in a block-structured language such as Pascal, Modula-2, Ada, or C; practical knowledge of programming methodologies; computer organization and data structures; and in-depth knowledge of at least two special topics from a list that includes compiling techniques, comparative programming languages, operating systems, and database systems.

A full-time student can complete the program in two calendar years. The course work is partitioned into four semesters of four courses each and an intensive summer session following the second academic year. We also offer the option of spending only the second year in full-time residence at Carnegie Mellon.

Curriculum

Fall Semester (1st Year)	Spring Semester (1st Year)
Software Systems Engineering	Software Creation and Maintenance
Formal Methods in Software Engineering	Software Analysis
Advanced System Design Principles	Software Project Management
Computer Science Elective	Computer Science Elective
Fall Semester (2nd Year)	**Spring Semester (2nd Year)**
Software Development Studio	Software Development Studio
Software Engineering Seminar	Software Engineering Seminar
Required Theory Course	Required Business Course
Advanced Computer Science Elective	Advanced Computer Science Elective
Summer (2nd Year)	
Software Development Studio	

During each of the first two semesters, students carry an academic load of three software engineering courses and one elective. The goal of the first year is to teach basic material on software engineering with an emphasis on programming-in-the-large and on software project management. The purpose of the two electives is to broaden the student's knowledge of computer science at the senior undergraduate level, or for some students, to bring that knowledge up to date.

We recognize that some professionals have already started taking courses elsewhere. Several universities already offer variants of the six first-year software engineering courses for credit via the SEI Video Dissemination Project. These courses are offered for graduate credit at CMU, videotaped, and made available for a modest cost to those universities that agree to supply a tutor and offer the courses for credit. In addition, many universities offer courses that satisfy the directed electives requirement. Although residence at CMU for the first year is preferred, it is possible under special circumstances to gain admission directly to the second year.

The second year, which must be taken in Pittsburgh, includes a seminar series, two required courses, two electives, and a software development studio that runs for two consecutive semesters and the following summer.

The software engineering seminar consists of a series of lectures by well-known software professionals and requires active participation by the students as well as the lecturers. Lecturers remain in residence for several days to provide students an opportunity for one-on-one interaction. The discussions, written assignments, and interactions provide an opportunity for students to practice and improve writing and presentation skills. The purpose of the required courses is to strengthen the student in two areas (computer science theory and business practices) that are useful to the practicing software engineer. The second year electives are required to further enhance specialized knowledge.

The most important component of the second year is the software development studio, which focuses on the planning, design, and evaluation of software products. The studio experience is the major difference between the Carnegie Mellon program and other software engineering degree programs. Often project courses in other programs involve the development of a piece of software using some idealized standard process, with emphasis on producing complete documentation. Our version of the project course is closer to the design studios that characterize architectural degree programs. Students have significant and continuing contact with faculty. The course is team-taught, with several faculty responsible for content and for working with the students. The faculty often work side by side with students, reviewing actual design and development work in progress, giving advice, and questioning student decisions. Additionally, the students do not stop with the creation of the software. A considerable amount of time is scheduled for an evaluation of the work produced, a plan for improvement of this work, and the execution of that plan. The students not only get a feel for exemplary software production, but they also learn how to determine the efficacy of designs and to engineer changes. In fact, many studio projects begin with existing software. Students work in a team to critique the design, change it, and further evaluate the changes that they made.

Master of Science in Software Engineering
Program at National University
Daniel P. Olivier, Intermetrics, Inc.
Ralph R. Hayward III, Inter-National Research Institute

National University is a private university accredited by the Western Association of Schools and Colleges with campuses located in California, Nevada, and Costa Rica. Undergraduate classes meet for forty-eight hours and graduate classes for forty hours of classroom instruction. Classes last four weeks and are offered primarily in the evenings to fit the working adult's schedule. National University is the third largest private university in California with over ten thousand students currently enrolled.

The Master of Science in Software Engineering program was started with a class of thirty students at the San Diego campus in April, 1985. Today over one hundred students are enrolled in the program at campuses including San Diego, San Jose, Sacramento, Irvine, Los Angeles, and Vista. As of December 1989, over four-hundred students have graduated from National University with the Master of Science in Software Engineering degree.

Planning for the program began in early 1984 when the faculty of the School of Engineering and Computer Science realized a need for a curriculum tailored to software engineering management. While there were several masters level programs in Information Systems to supply data processing management, few were available to educate software engineers in the more technical requirements associated with the development of complex software systems.

Faculty members and leaders from the local software industry formed a committee to define a program curriculum. First existing curriculums of other universities were studied with the software engineering programs at Seattle University and the Wang Institute selected as a model. A survey was then distributed to many of the companies whose employees attended National University to determine their needs for trained software engineers. Based on the study of the engineering programs and the results of this survey the committee established a curriculum that addressed practical application of modern software engineering principles. Ada was selected as the programming language to be used for all projects. Since the initial definition, the program had not changed until the winter quarter of 1989 when two Ada programming classes were removed from the core and made prerequisites. This change was made to provide more emphasis on software process and program management techniques rather than programming skills.

Team projects and real world scenarios are used throughout the curriculum to provide exposure to development problems common in industry. The final three classes are devoted to completion of an original student research project utilizing the software engineering methods presented. The majority of our students are practitioners in software engineering (84% according to a recent survey) who wish to learn ways to improve the software development expertise within their own companies. Instructors are composed mostly of adjunct faculty who work in local companies and are recognized experts within their fields.

Degree Requirements

The master of Science in Software Engineering degree requires the completion of 60 quarter units of graduate work, of which at least 45 quarter units must be completed in residence at National University. A total of 15 quarter units may be granted for previous graduate course work. The Software Engineering Project courses must be completed in residence.

Program Requirements

Candidates for the program must have: (1) a Bachelor of Science degree in Computer Science and successful completion of CS 521A and CS 521B or their equivalents, or (2) a Bachelor of Business Administration degree with elective emphasis in Information Systems and successful completion of CS 521A and CS 521B or equivalent. Students with other undergraduate degrees must complete prerequisite courses or verify equivalent work experience by satisfactory completion of a placement examination.

Prerequisite Courses (25 quarter units)

CS	314C	C PROGRAMMING
CS	315C	DATA STRUCTURES IN C
CS	418	PRINCIPLES OF HARDWARE ORGANIZATION
CS	422C	PRINCIPLES OF DATABASE SYSTEMS
CS	423A	OPERATING SYSTEM THEORY AND DESIGN
CS	431A	INTRODUCTION TO Ada
CS	431B	ADVANCED Ada

Core Courses (60 quarter units)

CS	620A	PRINCIPLES OF SOFTWARE ENGINEERING
CS	622	ADVANCED SOFTWARE ENGINEERING
CS	626	VERIFICATION AND VALIDATION TECHNIQUES
CS	624A	PRINCIPLES OF HARDWARE AND SOFTWARE INTEGRATION
CS	624B	SYSTEMS SOFTWARE
CS	624C	NETWORKED COMPUTING SYSTEMS
CS	623A/B	DATA BASE MANAGEMENT I AND II
CS	625A	EXPERT SYSTEMS
CS	627A/B/C	SOFTWARE ENGINEERING PROJECT I, II, AND III

Panel Discussion:
Industry-Academic Cooperation in
Software Engineering Training and Continuing Education

Moderator:

George Smith
Motorola Inc.
Schaumburg, Illinois

Panel Members:

Dr. A. Frank Ackerman
Consultant to AT&T Bell Laboratories
Whippany, New Jersey

George N. Arnovick
Professor, Computer Science
Director, Technical Research Center
Graduate School
California State University
Chico, California

W. J. "Gus" Radzyminski
Training Coordinator
Integration and System Product Division
Eastman Kodak Company
Rochester, New York

George Sanders
Training Manager
Motorola Training and Education Center
Schaumburg, Illinois.

Position papers submitted by the panelists follow. Dr. Ackermann was
unable to provide a paper in time for publication in these proceedings.

Position Paper:
Industry-Academic Cooperation in Software Engineering Training and Education

George N. Arnovick Professor,
Computer Science
Director, Technical Research Center,
Graduate School
California State University, Chico, CA

My comments as a panelist on the SEI Panel on Industry-Academic cooperation to be held at the Fourth SEI Conference on Software Engineering Education, Pittsburgh PA, April 2-3, 1990 will address two areas of concern for SE training: (1) the need for a formalized student co-op experience with government and private sector organizations; and (2) how academia can assist SE education/training on a continuous bases with organizations.

SE Co-op Programs

In addition to a University SE curriculum program that includes an experience component such as design labs, or other designated hands-on project activities, a more formal arrangement made with a government or private sector company to provide a one semester, or two quarter session student co-op experience will have an assigned number of unit credits. The Computer Science department at CSUC requires a formal evaluation of the student's co-op activity by the management of the organization the student worked in. If the student elects to receive academic unit credit, they must submit a written report which is graded by a faculty member.

Many co-op programs for computer science students do not include

An Emerging Vision of Software Engineering

W.J. Gus Radzyminski
Integration and Systems Product Division
Eastman Kodak Company

To compete successfully in a global marketplace, software engineers will need to bring to industry an understanding of many complex issues and possess multiple and adaptable strengths or attributes. Industry looks to institutions of higher learning for the equipping of individuals with the basic skills and awareness needed so that even new employees can contribute to progress and attainment of organizational goals. So what is industry looking for in software engineers? Let me suggest 4 target areas:

1. Awareness of software marketing and support
2. A sense of software's strategic differentiation potential
3. People skills
4. Execution skills

Taking note of the Biblical maxim that the last shall be first let me amplify these points in reverse order.

Execution skills. This is perhaps the easiest to comprehend - its predictable. Industry needs engineers who can produce software on time, quality assured, within costs. Obviously this means they have design skills, some hardware expertise, systems integration understanding, knowledge of software project management, development skills, concern with reliability and quality. There is a growing interest in multimedia exposure (document, video and voice). Even though "tools" change, industry wants software engineers to come with a fairly full tool box. While you may argue to what degree this is done, the point holds no surprise.

SE experience. The student is assigned a task as a working member of a software design or development team and quite frequently does not participate in formal SE processes. This lack of SE experience is attributed to either not including co-op students in SE activities as a matter of policy, or the organization does not practice SE.

In order to create the proper SE experience environment, articulation and agreements are needed between academia and the cooperating industry. These arrangements should clearly define the SE activity, its relationship to the co-op student, and the opportunity to work in an SE environment. Academic units are then able to advise their students in terms of working at specific organizations, and their expectations with respect to SE life cycle participation as a learning experience.

Academia's Role In SE Training In Industry

Computer Science departments should be encouraged to contact industry that have co-op programs and determine if SE training is needed. Based on the requirements of industry, training programs can be set up by experienced SE faculty. This sort of service can also be extended to industry and government that normally do not have co-op programs with Universities.

People Skills. Again, little surprise. Software development today is not a hacker's position. Software engineers must be interpersonally adept. They must be flexible, team players, able to focus on a target, negotiate difference and get commitment to doing the right job. However, I would suggest that the interpersonal nature is going to increasingly include inter-cultural experiences because of software being developed in a distributed global environment. Certainly, software development will become increasingly intergenerational as the current generation of software engineers age and become the "older generation." Can you picture the discussions that will arise when someone says, "When I was a kid, we wrote software..." The values, work norms, and languages of different generations must be balanced in order to get the job done.

Strategic differentiation. This point is a bit of a departure from traditional industry-academic discussions. Industry needs software engineers who possess a sense of software's contribution as a strategic differentiation element. Organizations needing to enhance the distinctiveness of their products increasingly find more and more of the difference between competing products is in the value added of the software components. While not expecting neophyte engineers to possess the wisdom of the ages, software engineering graduates need exposure to business planning principles and marketplace competition. They should be able to conduct basic competitive analysis, evaluate strategic partnership opportunities, perform make/build assessment. In short, build a sound business case for their software engineering technical strategy.

And the last shall be first. Software marketing and support. In my own company, and I see this in true in many, many other corporations, there are strong and frequent reminders that every employee "owns" the company and must act accordingly. Decision making is being driven down as far as possible. Employees are being empowered and encouraged to act decisively on their own.

It is easy and rather natural for those of us with software engineering curricula interests to focus on the engineering skills, software quality metrics, tool box issues. It is not as easy to "sell" the point that a software engineering education should include some marketing and support education. Software engineers should learn about customer support, distribution of software, how market needs are determined, internationalization of products and markets, how products are sold both internally and externally. The full product life cycle cannot be overlooked. We must not produce myopic engineers. There is far, far more to software products than bug free code. Engineers should be exposed to all the key support and sales elements surrounding software products. When this happens, better "owners" emerge.

Is industry expecting too much of academia? After all, there is so little time, so much to do. I'm not suggesting that no one enters a software engineering program as an 18 or 19 year old and emerge 10 or 20 years later. Industry has responsibility to help your graduates along. Software entry and development programs are needed. There is no question about that. I am however, urging that in our proceeding today and in the future, we talk about the education of the "whole" engineer.

The position expressed in the presentation are the views of the presenter and not necessarily the views of Eastman Kodak Company.

Position Paper:
Industry-Academic Cooperation in Software Engineering Training and Education

George Sanders
Motorola, Inc

For the past several months I have spent a great deal of time analyzing the current state of affairs of software engineering within and without Motorola Inc. (a prosperous communications company of nearly 100,000 dedicated employees relatively new to the game of software engineering). My general conclusion as it relates to the theme of this conference is that academic institutions are involved in industrial software engineering education not by purpose, but through the individual activity of university professors who share some of their unfettered time with corporate education departments in a piecemeal process of industrial software engineering education. Industrial giants, the IBM's, AT&T's, and the Hewlett Packard's of the world, use the resources of academia to help spread the gospel of world class software engineering practices. The common practice is to hire a university staff member on a contract basis to help deliver courses in software education deemed necessary by the industrial entity. As effective as this practice may be, it is subject to several shortcomings which beg for a more structured and permanent solution to industrial software engineering education.

First and foremost, the process as it now stands is reactive. As we know from our collective experience with software life cycles and relative defect rates in industrial products, the farther upstream we deal with the gestalt process, product, or problem, the fewer defects we will have upon implementation. I would argue that we have not completed a suitable analysis of industrial software engineering education. If we were to graphically portray the "system" as it exists today, we would not be able to come up with DFD 0, the most basic representation of a system. As a result, we are already in the architecture phase of development, way down stream, providing the best solutions we can without understanding (or perhaps ignoring) the fundamental requirements of the system.

The second shortcoming of the current state of industrial software engineering education is that it tends to favor those companies that have some or all of the following attributes:

Geographical proximity to academic institutions well-equipped to support industrial requirements in software engineering education.

An educational infrastructure which supports the capability to hire contract instructors from academia.

A history of industrial software engineering education.

A history of industrial education.

Companies that are new to the field of software engineering, that are not geographically connected to the academic world of software engineering, or that do no have a history of industrial education are unlikely to benefit from academicians offering their services on a contract basis.

Finally, the informal "contract" relationship that exists between academia and industry relative to software engineering education leads us to believe, inappropriately, I think, that industry and academia are joined together in a mutual software engineering education process. I suggest that before we can feel comfortable with the state of software engineering education in the United States, industry and academia need to establish a formal relationship which addresses the issue on an academic-wide and industry-wide basis.

Vol. 379: A. Kreczmar, G. Mirkowska (Eds.), Mathematical Foundations of Computer Science 1989. Proceedings, 1989. VIII, 605 pages. 1989.

Vol. 380: J. Csirik, J. Demetrovics, F. Gécseg (Eds.), Fundamentals of Computation Theory. Proceedings, 1989. XI, 493 pages. 1989.

Vol. 381: J. Dassow, J. Kelemen (Eds.), Machines, Languages, and Complexity. Proceedings, 1988. VI, 244 pages. 1989.

Vol. 382: F. Dehne, J.-R. Sack, N. Santoro (Eds.), Algorithms and Data Structures. WADS '89. Proceedings, 1989. IX, 592 pages. 1989.

Vol. 383: K. Furukawa, H. Tanaka, T. Fujisaki (Eds.), Logic Programming '88. Proceedings, 1988. VII, 251 pages. 1989 (Subseries LNAI).

Vol. 384: G. A. van Zee, J. G. G. van de Vorst (Eds.), Parallel Computing 1988. Proceedings, 1988. V, 135 pages. 1989.

Vol. 385: E. Börger, H. Kleine Büning, M. M. Richter (Eds.), CSL '88. Proceedings, 1988. VI, 399 pages. 1989.

Vol. 386: J.E. Pin (Ed.), Formal Properties of Finite Automata and Applications. Proceedings, 1988. VIII, 260 pages. 1989.

Vol. 387: C. Ghezzi, J. A. McDermid (Eds.), ESEC '89. 2nd European Software Engineering Conference. Proceedings, 1989. VI, 496 pages. 1989.

Vol. 388: G. Cohen, J. Wolfmann (Eds.), Coding Theory and Applications. Proceedings, 1988. IX, 329 pages. 1989.

Vol. 389: D. H. Pitt, D. E. Rydeheard, P. Dybjer, A. M. Pitts, A. Poigné (Eds.), Category Theory and Computer Science. Proceedings, 1989. VI, 365 pages. 1989.

Vol. 390: J.P. Martins, E.M. Morgado (Eds.), EPIA 89. Proceedings, 1989. XII, 400 pages. 1989 (Subseries LNAI).

Vol. 391: J.-D. Boissonnat, J.-P. Laumond (Eds.), Geometry and Robotics. Proceedings, 1988. VI, 413 pages. 1989.

Vol. 392: J.-C. Bermond, M. Raynal (Eds.), Distributed Algorithms. Proceedings, 1989. VI, 315 pages. 1989.

Vol. 393: H. Ehrig, H. Herrlich, H.-J. Kreowski, G. Preuß (Eds.), Categorical Methods in Computer Science. VI, 350 pages. 1989.

Vol. 394: M. Wirsing, J.A. Bergstra (Eds.), Algebraic Methods: Theory, Tools and Applications. VI, 558 pages. 1989.

Vol. 395: M. Schmidt-Schauß, Computational Aspects of an Order-Sorted Logic with Term Declarations. VIII, 171 pages. 1989. (Subseries LNAI).

Vol. 396: T. A. Berson, T. Beth (Eds.), Local Area Network Security. Proceedings, 1989. IX, 152 pages. 1989.

Vol. 397: K. P. Jantke (Ed.), Analogical and Inductive Inference. Proceedings, 1989. IX, 338 pages. 1989. (Subseries LNAI).

Vol. 398: B. Banieqbal, H. Barringer, A. Pnueli (Eds.), Temporal Logic in Specification. Proceedings, 1987. VI, 448 pages. 1989.

Vol. 399: V. Cantoni, R. Creutzburg, S. Levialdi, G. Wolf (Eds.), Recent Issues in Pattern Analysis and Recognition. VII, 400 pages. 1989.

Vol. 400: R. Klein, Concrete and Abstract Voronoi Diagrams. IV, 167 pages. 1989.

Vol. 401: H. Djidjev (Ed.), Optimal Algorithms. Proceedings, 1989. VI, 308 pages. 1989.

Vol. 402: T. P. Bagchi, V. K. Chaudhri, Interactive Relational Database Design. XI, 186 pages. 1989.

Vol. 403: S. Goldwasser (Ed.), Advances in Cryptology – CRYPTO '88. Proceedings, 1988. XI, 591 pages. 1990.

Vol. 404: J. Beer, Concepts, Design, and Performance Analysis of a Parallel Prolog Machine. VI, 128 pages. 1989.

Vol. 405: C. E. Veni Madhavan (Ed.), Foundations of Software Technology and Theoretical Computer Science. Proceedings, 1989. VIII, 339 pages. 1989.

Vol. 407: J. Sifakis (Ed.), Automatic Verification Methods for Finite State Systems. Proceedings, 1989. VII, 382 pages. 1990.

Vol. 408: M. Leeser, G. Brown (Eds.) Hardware Specification, Verification and Synthesis: Mathematical Aspects. Proceedings, 1989. VI, 402 pages. 1990.

Vol. 409: A. Buchmann, O. Günther, T. R. Smith, Y.-F. Wang (Eds.), Design and Implementation of Large Spatial Databases. Proceedings, 1989. IX, 364 pages. 1990.

Vol. 410: F. Pichler, R. Moreno-Diaz (Eds.), Computer Aided Systems Theory – EUROCAST '89. Proceedings, 1989. VII, 427 pages. 1990.

Vol. 411: M. Nagl (Ed.), Graph-Theoretic Concepts in Computer Science. Proceedings, 1989. VII, 374 pages. 1990.

Vol. 412: L. B. Almeida, C. J. Wellekens (Eds.), Neural Networks. Proceedings, 1990. IX, 276 pages. 1990.

Vol. 413: R. Lenz, Group Theoretical Methods in Image Processing. VIII, 139 pages. 1990.

Vol. 414: A.Kreczmar, A. Salwicki, M. Warpechowski, LOGLAN '88 – Report on the Programming Language. X, 133 pages. 1990.

Vol. 415: C. Choffrut, T. Lengauer (Eds.), STACS 90. Proceedings, 1990. VI, 312 pages. 1990.

Vol. 416: F. Bancilhon, C. Thanos, D. Tsichritzis (Eds.), Advances in Database Technology – EDBT '90. Proceedings, 1990. IX, 452 pages. 1990.

Vol. 417: P. Martin-Löf, G. Mints (Eds.), COLOG-88. International Conference on Computer Logic. Proceedings, 1988. VI, 338 pages. 1990.

Vol. 419: K. Weichselberger, S. Pöhlmann, A Methodology for Uncertainty in Knowledge-Based Systems, 1989. VIII, 136 pages. 1990. (Subseries LNAI).

Vol. 420: Z. Michalewicz (Ed.), Statistical and Scientific Database Management, V SSDBM. Proceedings, 1990. V, 256 pages. 1990.

Vol. 421: T. Onodera, S. Kawai, A Formal Model of Visualization in Computer Graphics Systems. X, 100 pages. 1990.

Vol. 423: L. E. Deimel (Ed.), Software Engineering Education. Proceedings, 1990. VI, 164 pages. 1990.